AA

...*focus on*...

Bath and Bristol

AA Publishing

Produced by AA Publishing
© The Automobile Association 1998
Maps © The Automobile Association 1998

First published 1998

Published by AA Publishing (a trading name of Automobile
Association Developments Limited, whose registered office is
Norfolk House, Priestley Road, Basingstoke, Hampshire RG24 9NY;
registered number 1878835).

ISBN 0 7495 1815 4

A CIP catalogue record for this book is available from
the British Library

Colour separation by Pace Colour Ltd, Southampton

Printed and bound in Italy by Stige, Turin

Find out more about AA Publishing and the wide range of services
the AA provides by visiting our Web site at www.theaa.co.uk.

BATH, BRISTOL AND BEYOND

The countryside which extends eastwards from the famous centres of Bath and Bristol encompasses a wide range of landscapes and attractions for the visitor. The historic seafaring city of Bristol contrasts in size and style with its elegant neighbour Bath, whose fame is founded on its hot springs, unique in Britain. Linking the two is the Bristol and Bath Cycleway, providing a leisurely way to see the local sights and wildlife. The Mendip Hills lie to the south, stretching right across Somerset from Weston-Super-Mare to Frome, and encompassing the popular tourist attractions at Cheddar and Wookey Hole. This area is rich in barrows and hill-forts dating from the Bronze and Iron Ages, and near by is Glastonbury, site of the legend of the Holy Grail.

Further north are the ancient market towns of Malmesbury and Tetbury with their graceful buildings, many in the famous mellow-coloured Cotswold Stone. Cirencester is proud of its Roman history; the town was strategically positioned at the junction of the Fosse Way and Ermin Way, and traces of Corinium in its prime are still visible in the outline of an 8,000-seat amphitheatre to the west of the town. The countryside around the Marlborough Downs is home to many mysterious shapes and sights: impenetrable Silbury Hill, the sarsen stones of Avebury, and a veritable herd of white horses cut into the chalk. Perhaps the most famous of these is found on the far side of Salisbury Plain, at Westbury, with the ancient hill-fort of Bratton Camp close by.

The area is rich in delightful villages, such as Nunney, Castle Combe and Frampton on Severn, and there are many grand houses and excellent gardens – including Longleat, Great Chalford Manor, Dyrham Park and Lacock Abbey. Railway enthusiasts will enjoy the East Somerset Railway, located near Shepton Mallet, and the Dean Forest Railway, just north of Lydney in Gloucestershire. You can even picnic at a restored railway station, at Tintern Parva.

gazetteer

▷ The manor house of this Coln Valley village was the home of Arthur Gibbs, author of best-selling classic *A Cotswold Village* (1898).
(See also Walk: Coln Valley, pages 32–3.)

▷ Amesbury stands on the edge of Salisbury Plain; the buildings are mostly small-scale modern, but the large medieval church is partly 13th century. There are big army camps on either side.
(See also Stonehenge, page 79; Woodhenge, page 93.)

▷ To enter this unique village and observe its daily life, apparently unaffected by the immense Neolithic stone circle within which it partly stands, is to feel the centuries concertina into timelessness. The circle, with its gaunt stones and its vast bank and ditch, was probably in use as a major ceremonial centre from *c*2500 BC. In the early Middle Ages, however, with the arrival of the first Christian chapel at Avebury, villagers set about burying some of the pagan stones. By the 18th century, when the village was expanding, other stones were broken up

ABLINGTON
GLOUCESTERSHIRE. VILLAGE OFF B4425, 1 MILE (2KM) NW OF BIBURY

AMESBURY
WILTSHIRE. TOWN ON A345, 7 MILES (11KM) N OF SALISBURY

AVEBURY
WILTSHIRE. VILLAGE ON A3461, 6 MILES (10KM) W OF MARLBOROUGH

The stone circle at Avebury

JOHN AUBREY

In 1663 the diarist John Aubrey wrote that the prehistoric site of Avebury '...does as much exceed Stonehenge in greatness as a cathedral does a parish church'. The 28-acre (11.3-ha) complex is indeed larger and arguably more impressive than its more famous and now, sadly, somewhat tawdry sister.

Alexander Keiller Museum
Tel: *01672 539250*

Avebury Manor
6 miles (9.5km) W of Marlborough; from A4 take A4361/84003
Tel: *01672 539250*

AVONMOUTH
Bristol. Town on A403, 6 miles (10km) NW of Bristol

AXBRIDGE
Somerset. Small town off A371, 2 miles (3km) W of Cheddar

and these squarish blocks of sarsen can be seen in several of the buildings, including the old school, Silbury House and the Methodist chapel. As recently as the early 1960s the National Trust seriously considered demolishing parts of the village within the circle, including the manorial aisled barn that now houses the Museum of Wiltshire Folk Life. The uneasy partnership between village and prehistoric settlement seems now to have settled into mutual forbearance, with the thatched pub plying its trade in the shadow of the stones. The church, of Saxon and Norman origins, is remarkable for its south doorway, font and rood screen, and sits prettily within the Elizabethan manor house just outside the earthwork. Other attractive houses both inside and outside the circle are built of brick, flint or cob; some are timber-framed, and several thatched.

▶ This is one of the most important prehistoric sites in Europe, and was built before Stonehenge. In the midst of it is the pretty village of Avebury, surrounded by circles of massive sarsen stones and an impressive circular embankment and ditch. An avenue of great stones leads to the site, which must have been a place of great religious significance. The small museum has recently been refurbished and contains many new exhibits. It is named after Alexander Keiller, the first archaeologist to analyse the site in a modern way. It shows finds from Avenury and from Windmill Hill, a Neolithic causewayed enclosure about 1½ miles (2.5km) away, which is also part of the National Trust property. Educational facilities are provided.
  Open all year, daily. Closed Xmas and New Year.

▶ Avebury Manor has a monastic origin, and has been much altered since then. The present buildings date from the early 16th century, with notable Queen Anne alterations and Edwardian renovation. The flower gardens contain medieval walls, and there are examples of topiary.
  Garden and Manor open Mar–Nov, certain days.

▶ Avonmouth developed at the mouth of the Avon in the later 19th century because ships were becoming larger and could not get up the narrow river to Bristol. From 1868 docks were constructed, and a big smelting plant followed. The docks still flourish, recently on the south bank as well, and there is much industry.

▶ Axbridge was once a large town, and has a market place and town hall of 1833. The church is 15th century, very fine, with a fan vault and unusual plaster ceiling of 1636.

gazetteer

Visitors admire the sundial
and small box hedges at
Barnsley House

Nothing to do with King John or with hunting, this jettied and timber-framed house was built around 1500. It gives a good indication of the wealth of the merchants of that time and is now a museum of local history, with old photographs, paintings and items such as the town stocks and constables' staves.

Open Etr–Sep, daily (afternoons).

King John's Hunting Lodge
THE SQUARE
TEL: 01934 732012

Barnsley is surely one of the prettiest stone villages in the Cotswolds. Barnsley House keeps its charms hidden until the last moment, but once the abrupt entrance drive has been negotiated the immediate and lasting impression is one of harmony. The honey-coloured Queen Anne house stands serenely amid 4 acres (1.6ha) of intimate garden enclosures interrupted by a sweeping lawn with softly coloured herbaceous borders.

Near to the house on the western side is a knot garden, its little box hedges set in gravel in the manner of the formal *parterres* of the 16th and 17th centuries. In the 1960s the owner moved a temple dating from 1770 from Fairford Park to the south-east corner of the garden, thus creating a peaceful vista leading over the lily pond, through two iron gates flanked by cypresses, to a wall fountain at the other end. Alongside the potager, or decorative kitchen garden, runs a wonderful laburnum tunnel.

This potager, inspired by the one at the Château de Villandry, in the Loire valley, is a remarkable creation. Brick paths criss-cross the area, and the beds themselves are planted with red and green varieties of lettuce and other vegetables, while sweet peas grow close to gooseberries and onions, cabbages, lavender and strawberries. Perhaps the layout is typical of Barnsley House garden as a whole – a charming mixture of nonchalance and formality.

Garden open all year, certain days.

BARNSLEY HOUSE
BARNSLEY, GLOUCESTERSHIRE
4 MILES (6.5KM) NE OF
CIRENCESTER
TEL: 01285 740281

BATH

SOMERSET. CITY ON A4, 11 MILES (18KM) SE OF BRISTOL

Bath is the most elegant town in the country, with acres of handsome Georgian buildings in the creamy orange local stone and surrounded by small green hills. The town has always been based on its natural hot springs, the largest producing a million litres a day of red-stained hot water. The Romans built their baths around the spring, with a temple dedicated both to Minerva and to the Celtic water goddess

Sulis, providing a mixture of physical healing and spiritual refreshment, doubtless, as later, relieved with more social amusements.

The Roman baths were rediscovered in the later 19th century, and can be seen along with the little medieval King's Bath and displays of finds which include Roman sculpture and Roman curses inscribed on little rolls of lead which were thrown into the spring.

Medieval Bath was small, with a big monastery, whose large and handsome early 16th-century church survives as Bath Abbey, fan-vaulted and with a famous west front.

The 17th-century town was promoted as a spa, and really took off from 1725, becoming the most fashionable resort in the country. Present-day Bath is the stylish town created for those who came to bathe and to drink the water in the Georgian period.

Two people heavily influenced the town: 'Beau' Nash, the official Master of Ceremonies for 50 years who made the resort genteel, and the architect John Wood, who designed many areas of Bath including the Circus (1754), the large circular terrace. His son designed the Royal Crescent (see page 10) and the Assembly Rooms in the 1760s, while Robert Adam produced Pulteney Bridge at the same time. Other notable buildings include the Guildhall (1776) and the Pump Room (1789), but fine as these individual buildings are, it is Bath as a whole which impresses: miles of Georgian houses, mostly in terraces, looking much as they did when Jane Austen or Gainsborough visited. Royal

Above: Royal Crescent is a graceful curve of 30 houses

Opposite: The Roman baths, with Bath Abbey in the background

Victoria Park (laid out from 1830) and the Botanic Gardens in the north-west part are fine Victorian additions to the town, although by then it had ceased to be fashionable. The best view of the city is from the wooded ridge to the south.

Two of Jane Austen's novels, *Northanger Abbey* and *Persuasion*, are partly set in Regency Bath and give a good picture of the social life then, as do the Assembly Rooms and the Museum of Costume (see below).

Today Bath attracts visitors from all over the world, and has masses of smart shops. The annual summer music festival holds concerts in many of the Georgian buildings, and the Holbourne of Menstrie Museum (in a hotel of 1796) and the Victoria Art Gallery have temporary exhibitions as well as their permanent displays. The Building of Bath Museum (see below) has details of the construction of the Georgian town. Bath is always bustling and always beautiful.

The Building of Bath Museum
COUNTESS OF HUNTINGDON'S CHAPEL, THE VINEYARDS, THE PARAGON (LEAVE M4 AT JUNCTION 18, TAKE A46 TOWARDS CITY CENTRE, THEN A4; TAKE 2ND EXIT AT MINI-ROUNDABOUT)
TEL: 01225 333895

This new museum relates the fascinating story of how Georgian Bath was created. The exhibition depicts elegant society life in 'Beau' Nash's spa resort and explains how the splendid houses were constructed, from the laying of the first foundation stone to the last coat of paint. Exhibits include full-scale 'hands-on' reconstructions, collections of original tools, architectural fragments and a series of spectacular models, including the huge historic city model where famous buildings light up at the touch of a button. After a visit, the street scene outside seems like an extension of the exhibitions: visitors stop and study doors and windows, peer down into basements or up at the chimney tops. The Building of Bath Museum provides an excellent introduction for any visitor to Bath.

Open Feb–Nov, certain days.

Museum of Costume
4 CIRCUS
TEL: 01225 477789

The Museum of Costume is one of the largest and most prestigious collections of fashionable dress for men, women and children, covering the late 16th century to the present day. It is housed in Bath's famous 18th-century Assembly Rooms designed by John Woods the Younger in 1771. A special feature of the museums is the exhibition of wedding dresses.

Open all year, daily. Closed Xmas.

No 1 Royal Crescent
TEL: 01225 428126

Bath is very much a Georgian city, but most of its houses have naturally altered over the years to suit changing tastes and lifestyles. Built in 1768 by John Wood the Elder, No 1 Royal Crescent has been restored to look as it would have done some 200 years ago. Two floors are furnished as they might have been in the 18th century, with

Elegant figures in Bath's Museum of Costume

pictures, china and furniture of the period, and there is also an interesting kitchen. Note the first-floor windows, which are the original length; all the others in the Royal Crescent were lengthened downwards in the 19th century. The house was once the home of the Duke of York, famed for marching his 10,000 men uphill and down again.

Open Feb–Nov, certain days. Closed Good Friday.

Roman Baths & Pump Room
Abbey Church Yard
Tel: 01225 477785

The descent to the Roman baths is a step back in time. The remains give a vivid impression of life neary 2,000 years ago. The baths, built next to Britain's only hot spring, served the sick and the pilgrims visiting the ancient Temple of Sulis Minerva. The spring was a sacred site lying within the courtyard of the Temple. Votive offerings and temple treasures discovered during excavations of the spring can be seen in the museum display. Today, the Temple Courtyard is beneath the Pump Room, a popular meeting place in the 18th century when Bath was the leading resort for fashionable society. Inside the present Pump Room there is now a restaurant where morning coffee, lunches and teas are served. The hot spa water can also be sampled.

Open all year, daily.

Royal Photographic Society
THE OCTAGON, MILSOM ST
TEL: 01225 462841

The Octagon was built in 1796 as a chapel, but is now the headquarters of the world's oldest photographic society. A huge collection of cameras, the first photograph and other classics are displayed. Temporary exhibitions often feature leading examples of contemporary work. A variety of workshops, seminars and talks are held throughout the year.

Open all year, daily. Closed Xmas.

Sally Lunn's Refreshment House & Museum
4 NORTH PARADE PASSAGE
TEL: 01225 461634

The history of this Tudor building can be traced back to Roman times. It is the oldest house in Bath, and became a popular meeting place in the 18th century. In the cellars, a fascinating museum reveals the findings of recent excavations. Here too is the original kitchen, with its faggot oven, Georgian cooking range and a collection of baking utensils. The traditional 'Sally Lunn' is still served in the restaurant; it is a bread like the French brioche, made with eggs and butter, and popularly believed to have been named after its first maker, who came to Bath in 1680. The last week in October each year is the Bath

The quaint bowed shop window at Sally Lunn's Refreshment House

'Open Free Museum Week'.
    Open all year, daily. Closed Xmas and New Year.

▸ The 'capital' of the Severnside region of scattered farms known as the Vale of Berkeley, this pleasant town is dominated by the extensive and well-preserved castle (see below), with its keep, great hall, state apartments and cell where Edward II was murdered in 1327. An interesting church is set within the castle bounds. The Jenner Museum (see below) commemorates the pioneer of smallpox vaccines.

▸ Secluded Berkeley Castle, near the banks of the River Severn, was the site of one of the most infamous of all medieval murders. By 1327, Queen Isabella and her lover, the powerful baron Roger Mortimer, had wrested the crown from Edward II and were running the country. Edward was taken secretly to Berkeley Castle in April 1327, where attempts were made to starve him to death. Dead animals were thrown into a pit in his room in the hope that the smell would make him sicken and die. But Edward was a strong man and Isabella saw that more drastic measures were necessary. In September, according to tradition, the unfortunate king was murdered by having a red-hot poker thrust into his bowels.
    Although the chamber in which Edward is said to have been imprisoned remains, most of the castle dates from the mid-14th century and has survived essentially unchanged since then. It is a great palace-fortress built around a courtyard. Many of Berkeley's rooms are open to visitors, displaying some beautiful furnishings. One room contains furniture said to have belonged to Sir Francis Drake, while the magnificent Great Hall has a superb timber roof dating from the 14th century.
    Open Etr–Sep most days, Sun afternoons in Oct.

▸ This beautiful Georgian house was the home of Edward Jenner, the discoverer of a vaccine against smallpox. The house and garden, with its Temple of Vaccinia, are much as they were in Jenner's day. The displays record Jenner's life as an 18th-century country doctor, his work on vaccination and his interest in natural history. He is buried in the nearby church, which also has some fine monuments to the Berkeley family. To commemorate the bicentenary (1996) of Jenner's first vaccination experiment a permanent new exhibition on immunology (the medical science he founded) was opened on the first floor. This uses text, CD-ROMs and computer games to entertain and educate about this important branch of medicine.
    Open Apr–Oct, certain days.

BERKELEY
GLOUCESTERSHIRE. VILLAGE ON B4509, 5 MILES (8KM) W OF DURSLEY

Berkeley Castle
ON B4509 1½ MILES (2.5KM) W OF A38
TEL: 01453 810332

Berkeley's towers appear in martial pride,
Menacing all around the champaign wide
Right famous as the seat of barons bold
And valiant earls whose great exploits are told.
MICHAEL DRAYTON (1563–1611)

Jenner Museum
CHURCH LANE. FOLLOW THE TOURIST SIGNS FROM THE A38 TO THE TOWN CENTRE, TURN LEFT INTO HIGH STREET AND LEFT AGAIN INTO CHURCH LANE
TEL: 01453 810631

BIDDESTONE

WILTSHIRE. VILLAGE OFF A420, 4 MILES (6KM) W OF CHIPPENHAM

▶ Stone houses and cottages cluster around a green, with a village pond. The church dates from Norman and later periods, and still has Georgian box pews and a gallery.

BLAGDON

SOMERSET. VILLAGE ON A368, 7 MILES (11KM) NE OF AXBRIDGE

▶ Blagdon is a large village set on the lower slope of Blagdon Hill, on the edge of the Mendips, with Blagdon Lake (a reservoir built in 1900) below. It features a substantial 15th-century church tower.

BRADFORD-ON-AVON

WILTSHIRE. TOWN ON A363, 3 MILES (5KM) NW OF TROWBRIDGE

The 'blind house' on the 13th-century bridge at Bradford-on-Avon was originally built as a chapel

▶ One of England's prettiest stone small towns, with steep streets and the River Avon completing the picture. The 17th-century stone bridge and big Victorian mill are reminders that the town was founded on woollen cloth manufacture. Many 17th- and 18th-century stone houses and cottages line the streets. There are three churches, the smallest of which (St Lawrence) is the most interesting – a tiny but complete Saxon church of the 8th–10th centuries, a rare survival.

The 14th-century Tithe Barn (see page 15) is large, built of stone, and 168ft (51m) long with an original roof. The Kennet and Avon Canal loops around the town, making an interesting walk. There is a local museum, and Barton Farm Country Park is set in the meadows.

Built during the Wars of the Roses, the manor is a beautiful, mellow, moated house which still has its great hall. It was restored in the 1920s. There is a small 13th-century church next to the house.

Open Apr–Oct, certain days.

The Tithe Barn stands on Barton Farm, which belonged to Shaftesbury Abbey. It was probably used to store general farm produce as well as tithes of hay and corn. The roof is of stone slates, supported outside by buttresses and inside by an impressive network of great beams and rafters.

Open all year, daily.

Bratton is a big village, tucked up under the edge of Salisbury Plain downs. There are several Georgian brick houses, and some older timber-framing. The brick Baptist chapel dates from 1734: the church is 15th-century. To the southwest is Bratton Camp, an Iron Age hillfort with massive banks. Close by, cut into the chalk, is the early 18th-century Westbury White Horse. (See also Westbury, page 88.)

Great Chalfield Manor
3 MILES (5KM) SW OF MELKSHAM
TEL: 01985 843600

Tithe Barn
BARTON FARM

BRATTON
WILTSHIRE. VILLAGE ON B3098, 3 MILES (5KM) E OF WESTBURY

The massive stone-built Tithe Barn at Bradford-on-Avon

A pleasant and undemanding stroll along the well-maintained towpaths of Bradford Canal and the river, with plenty of opportunities for refreshment breaks along the way

Grid ref: ST825607

INFORMATION

The walk is 3 miles (5km) long.
Level, easy walking on
good paths.
One stile, if extension walk
is taken.
Dogs should be kept on leads.
Pub and seasonal teashop at
Avoncliff; also teashop at Barton
Farm; pubs, restaurants and
teashops at Bradford-on-Avon
Picnic tables by the river at
Barton Farm.

START

The walk starts from the railway
station car park in scenic
Bradford-on-Avon.

DIRECTIONS

Go through the gap at the far end
of the car park, turn left along the
river bank across the open area
to a broad tarmac path which
runs parallel with the river. Follow
this path until it joins the canal
opposite a swing bridge. Turn
right along the canal bank, and
continue to a clearly marked right
turn leading down to the river. (To
reach the aqueduct at Avoncliff
continue along the path.) Turn
right and follow the river bank
towards Bradford. After climbing
the stile, keep to the right around
the pumping station and up to the
canal bank. Turn left at the swing
bridge and follow this path until it
leaves the canal bank and joins
the road. (At this point you may
take a detour to Bradford Lock by
crossing the road, turning right,
and then going through a gate on
the left. Retrace your steps and
re-cross the road.) Turn left along
the road for a short distance, then
turn left through a small gate and
head towards the tithe barn within

*A trip by barge along the canal
at Bradford-on-Avon*

Barton Farm Country Park, entering through the gate to the right of the beech tree. After visiting the barn, rejoin the river path, turn right and go under the railway bridge. Continue along the bank, and turn right beside the swimming pool to return to the car park.

WHAT TO LOOK OUT FOR

There is always something to see on the canal and river – narrowboats, dinghies, birdlife and anglers. At a right angle to the large Tithe Barn (see page 15) is its much smaller predecessor.

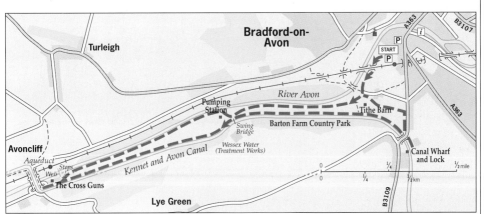

Bradford's Blind House

Originally used as a chapel, this tiny stone building on the ancient town bridge is thought to have become a prison at some time in the early 18th century. Such places were sometimes referred to as 'blind houses' because there were no windows and conditions inside were abominable. It is possible to obtain the key from a nearby shop and go inside.

A peaceful stretch of the river near Bradford-on-Avon

The famous SS Great Britain, now returned to Bristol where she was built in 1843

SS. GREAT BRITAIN

BRISTOL

CITY OFF M4/M5, 106 MILES (171KM) W OF LONDON

This huge city on the River Avon has been a port from medieval times, when it was almost as large as London. The medieval town was based around a bridge across the river, and traded with France, Spain, Portugal and Holland, importing many luxury goods such as wine, and exporting woollen cloth. Bombing in World War II removed many medieval buildings, but several medieval churches remain. The cathedral was the abbey church and still has the Norman chapter house and three gateways besides the church itself, which is later medieval with a very fine Lady Chapel. St Mary Redcliffe is considered the best medieval parish church in the country: 13th- and 14th-century, large, rich and intricate with a soaring spire.

The harbour was improved in the 13th century, and reached its present form with the floating harbour (always full of water) and basins in the early 19th century. It is no longer a commercial port (the docks are at the mouth of the Avon), but the docks still dominate the middle of the city and have become an attraction, with the Maritime Heritage Centre, Bristol Industrial Museum, ferries, occasional steam trains and most famously the SS *Great Britain*, Brunel's vast steam ship of 1843, now being fully restored. Harvey's Wine Cellars Museum is a reminder of one famous part of Bristol's trade. Some big 17th-century timber-framed houses and inns survive, and the Tudor Red Lodge has early furniture as well.

After a decline, Bristol again became the city with the second largest population in the country in the first half of the 18th century, and there are many Georgian houses still surviving, including squares and even a crescent. Queen Square is the most impressive, and Georgian House has been furnished as a museum of 18th-century life. John Wesley's chapel dates from 1739, and is the earliest Methodist building in the world.

The Exchange, built in the classical style of the 1740s, has earlier bronze pillars outside called Nails. This was the place where the merchants paid out – the origin of the phrase 'to pay on the nail'.

Bristol was on the early Great Western Railway, and part of Temple Meads Station is one of the earliest stations in the country, built in 1839 with castellated stone. Nineteenth-century Bristol processed tobacco and made chocolate, both industries being based on local imports. Soap and glass were also produced, blue glass being a Bristol speciality.

The town centre is very diverse, with many Victorian commercial buildings including a covered market, the big Victorian City Museum, and a mixture from Georgian to modern. The huge Gothic tower of the Wills Memorial Building (1925, part of the University) is a particular landmark. There are two theatres (one 18th-century) and a concert hall. Christmas Steps is lined with old buildings.

The docks are an excellent starting point for a tour of Bristol's attractions

The Clifton Suspension Bridge links the sheer limestone cliffs of the Avon Gorge

The best view of the city is from Cabot Tower, Brandon Hill. The little Gothic tower (1897) is a memorial to the great sailor who left from Bristol in 1496 to discover Newfoundland (he thought it was China).

Bristol today spreads across several hills, and, in contrast to its genteel neighbour, Bath, is a functional city, lively and cosmopolitan, but still very human despite its great size.

Clifton Suspension Bridge
CLIFTON. LINKS THE A4 WITH THE A369

▶ The majestic Clifton Suspension Bridge is Bristol's most famous landmark. It was designed by Isambard Kingdom Brunel in 1829, but was not finished until 1864. The bridge spans the Avon Gorge, some 245 feet (75m) above the river at high tide. It was considered one of the wonders of Victorian England, and still has the power to amaze visitors today. Brunel (1806–59) was the greatest designer and

wrought-iron architect of his day; he moved on from his triumphs with the Great Western Railway (including the design of Bristol Temple Meads Station) to build the transatlantic paddle steamer, the *Great Western*, launched from Bristol in 1837. He then superseded this with the SS *Great Britain*, the first ever iron ocean-going propellor-driven ship. The Bridge was his *pièce de résistance*, which sadly he did not live to see completed.

Adjacent to the Bridge is the Clifton Observatory, which houses the only camera obscura in England open to the public. A large concave dish is housed in a darkened room, providing a 360-degree view of the surrounding area. From here a tunnel leads to a natural cave which opens on the the side of the Avon Gorge.

A visit to the Clifton Suspension Bridge can be combined with a visit to Bristol Zoo on Clifton Down, with its gloriously landscaped grounds.Over 300 species of wildlife are showcased here, with recent additions including a gorilla island and a huge walk-through aviary. A visit to the Zoo helps to provide funds for the important wotk of conservation.

THE BRISTOL AND BATH CYCLEWAY

*S*tarting in the historic spa-town of Bath, this route makes use of the famous Bristol and Bath Cycleway. Constructed by the Bristol-based charity Sustrans, this was the first major urban cycle/pedestrian route in the country. The ride loops down through Keynsham and pretty villages, to return on the cycleway.

INFORMATION

Total Distance
21 miles (33.5km)

Difficulty
Moderate

OS Map
Landranger 1:50,000 sheet 172
(Bristol & Bath)

Tourist Information
Bath, tel: 01225 47710;
Bristol, tel: 01179 260767

Cycle Shops/Hire
Avon Valley Cyclery (repairs),
Bath, tel: 01225 497710;
John's Bikes, Bath, tel: 01225
334633; Woods Cycles,
Hanham, tel: 01179 352042;
Buggies and Bikes (repairs),
Keynsham,
tel: 01179 868184

Nearest Railway Station
Bath Spa

Refreshments
Bath has many pubs, cafes and
restaurants; Avon Valley Railway;
Keynsham has various pubs and
tea rooms; also good food at The
Compton pub, Compton Dando,
where there are facilities for
children.

START
Bath is situated on the A4, south-
east of Bristol. The route starts at

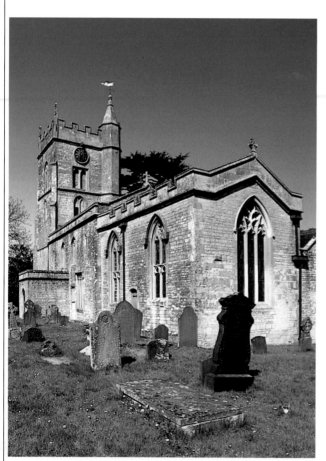

The church at Compton Dando

Pond-dipping at Willsbridge Mill

the Victoria Park play area, near the famous Royal Crescent, where there is usually plenty of on-street parking available.

DIRECTIONS

1. Head west from Victoria Park along the A4, towards Bristol. Go straight through the traffic lights by the Fina petrol station, and after a short distance bear left into Locksbrooke Road, signposted to the Bristol and Bath Railway Path. Follow this road through the industrial estate, across a mini roundabout, and past The Dolphin pub. A few yards further on reach the canal, and look out for a lock, a short way ahead on the left. As Johnson's newsagency comes into view, take the road on the left and turn immediately right on to the Bristol and Bath Cycleway.

2. You are now in a traffic-free zone, and can enjoy a lazy, level ride all the way to the Avon Valley Railway some 5 miles (8km)

further on. As a general rule, it is best to keep to the left. At intervals along the Cycleway, notice boards give information about wildlife. There are also rest points. At the Avon Valley Railway there are refreshment facilities, parking and toilets, as well as a display of railway memorabilia to be viewed.

3. Leave the railway, and head down the drive to the main road, to turn sharp right under the old railway bridge. At the roundabout, to visit Willsbridge Mill, bear right here, proceed down a dip and up the other side. About half-way up the rise there is a footpath off to the right which takes you straight into Willsbridge Mill. To rejoin the main route, leave the Mill and turn left down the hill, back to the roundabout. Bear right on to the A4175, signposted 'Keynsham', but take care – this road carries some very heavy traffic. Pedal across the valley floor passing the Cadbury factory on the right and the Portavon Marina, before

crossing the River Avon. Pedal up the rise past the railway station, and continue to the roundabout by the church of St John the Baptist. Turn left here, and first right into Charlton Road, signposted to Queen Charlton and Whitchurch. Follow the road out into open countryside, forking left to Woollard after 2 miles (3km). Turn left at the unmarked crossroads (with a bungalow on the opposite corner) into a small lane, taking care round the sharp bends at Wooscombe Bottom. Enjoy the views across the open country below and around you. There is a small car park if you need a breather.

4. Continue towards Compton Dando – enjoy the descent, but do take care; gravel and a number of sharp corners must be negotiated before you finally drop down into Compton Dando. Turn right out of Peppershell Lane into the village, going over the small hump-backed bridge. A little further on is The Compton Inn, and the village church is also worth exploring. After crossing the bridge take the first turning left, signposted to Burnett and Stanton Prior. Climb up Bathford Hill, away from the village, past the green into open countryside. After ½ mile (1km) take the left fork, dropping into the valley, and continue round the sharp bends at the bottom. Climb up the narrow land, and up the sharp rise into Burnett.

THE BRISTOL AND BATH CYCLEWAY

5. Continue to the crossroads and cross straight over the B3116 with great care, into Middlepiece Lane. Continue to a T-junction and turn left. In a short distance, go straight over the crossroads, towards Saltford. Enjoy the freewheel down the side of the wood, passing Lower Fields, and eventually turn right into Manor Road. At the end, turn right again, following the road round the residential area and down to the main road. Take care crossing (use the pelican crossing lights if necessary), and head left, straight down Beech Road. At the bottom turn right into the High Street, opposite Brunel's Tunnel House Hotel, and continue to The Bird in Hand pub. Go down the side of the pub and just under the railway bridge turn right, which leads back on to the cycle path.

6. Turn towards Bath, and retrace your route to the start at Victoria Park play area.

PLACES OF INTEREST

Willsbridge Mill

Willsbridge Mill, headquarters of the Avon Wildlife Trust, is a nature oasis just within the bounds of Bristol, and its buildings house many exhibitions and teaching facilities. It is a favourite destination for school parties, but these seldom occur at weekends. There are also many nature trails and 'outdoor experiments' which you can see in operation.

WHAT TO LOOK OUT FOR

The northern section of the disused railway line on this route, the Avon Walkway, passes through the Avon Valley Country Park.

Two quiet villages

Burnett, on the outskirts of Keynsham, has in its small area a wealth of old buildings which have been carefully looked after. Although one or two sport modern appendages, most retain the original exterior and roof. The village plan has remained unchanged for most of this century, even through the two world wars, when a local military base (now disused) was established near by. Compton Dando sits in the bottom of the valley, bisected by the River Chew. The church is sited some little way off the village centre, but the walk up Church Lane can bring a welcome relief from sitting in the saddle. The village dates back to medieval times, and the overall effect is on visitors is one of peace and tranquillity.

Inside the church at Castle Combe

Calne was once the centre of the Wiltshire bacon industry, with Harris's huge factory in the middle of the town. There are Georgian houses around the green, and 17th-century houses (including almshouses of 1682) near the big 15th-century church, built from the profits of the woollen cloth trade. Bowood House (see below) is part of an 18th-century mansion, with a museum and grounds which are some of the finest in the country.

The museum contains over 60 exhibits, which include cars from 1924–83, classic motorbikes, lawn mowers and memorabilia.
Open all year; closed Fri and Sat.

Originally built in 1624, the house was unfinished when it was bought by the first Earl of Shelbourne in 1754. He employed celebrated architects, notably Robert Adam, to complete the work, and what the visitor sees now is a handsome Georgian house. Adam's library is particularly admired, and also in the house is the laboratory where Dr Joseph Priestley discovered oxygen in 1774. There are fine paintings, sculptures, costumes and other displays. The chief glory of Bowood, however, is its 2,000-acre (810ha) expanse, 100 acres of which are pleasure gardens. They were laid out by 'Capability' Brown in the 1760s and are carpeted with daffodils, narcissi and bluebells in spring. The centrepiece is a lake, while terraces, roses, clipped yews and sculptures are a perfect complement to the house. There is also a hermit's cave, a temple and cascade; and for children there is a huge adventure playground. Please ring for details of special events.
Open end Mar–end Oct, daily. Rhododendron gardens (separate entrance off A342) open 6 weeks during May & June.

An especially pretty village set in a hollow on the southern edge of the Cotswolds, Castle Combe owes its name to the fortification built here, first by the Romans, then by the Saxons and finally by Walter de Dunstanville, a Norman. Little remains of his castle but he has a splendid tomb in the church, which is itself a fine example of Gothic architecture, built largely on the wealth of the local clothiers. Near by is the 15th-century market cross, its hipped stone roof supported by four heavy posts. The honeyed-stone weavers' cottages run down the hill to the By Brook. The bigger houses include the old manor house, now a hotel. The old court house may be distinguished by its overhung, half-timbered upper storey. Behind is the old gaol, a wattle-and-daub building. There is a stone dovecote and, beyond, the triple-arched packhorse bridge over the By Brook.

CALNE
WILTSHIRE. TOWN ON A4, 5 MILES (8KM) E OF CHIPPENHAM

Atwell-Wilson Motor Museum
'DOWNSIDE', STOCKLEY LANE. OFF A4 AT QUEMERFORD
TEL: 01249 813119

Bowood House and Gardens
OFF A4, IN DERRY HILL VILLAGE
TEL: 01249 812102

Robert Adam's original drawings for what is now the sculpture gallery show pens for wild animals, and family records detail the sad demise of an orang-utan at Christmas in 1768. Jeremy Bentham, the philosopher, visiting the house in 1781, spoke of going to stroke the leopard!

CASTLE COMBE
WILTSHIRE
VILLAGE OFF B4039, 5 MILES (8KM) NW OF CHIPPENHAM

*C*hew Valley Lake is one of the largest artificial lakes in the south-west of England. It provides an important over-wintering site for wildfowl, and as the lake is popular with anglers and sailors as well as picnickers.

HOW TO GET THERE

Follow the B3114 from Chew Magna to Chew Stoke, turning left before a tiny chapel on to a road signposted for Bishop Sutton. Follow the road for 1 mile

Chew Valley Lake, a peaceful picnic site with splendid views

(1.5km) with the lake to your right, until you reach the entrance to the picnic site.

FACILITIES

The Chew Valley Lake Information Centre (open daily) provides information on the nature trail, which follows the east bank of

the lake. Boat hire and fishing permits are available from Woodford Lodge.
Several picnic tables are set on the edge of the lake.
Tearoom, gift shop, and toilets with facilities for disabled people.

THE SITE

Chew Valley Lake is a peaceful, grassy picnic venue with pleasant views across the water to the distant Mendip Hills. Its excellent facilities make it a pleasant spot for a stroll along the nature trail beside the lake, or for enjoying some refreshments while watching the numerous wading birds, ducks and herons.

Tucked away from the road, on the north bank of an extensive lake formed by the river Chew, the site offers a choice between grassy banks and shady chestnut trees. The lake is renowned for its wildlife, sailing and fishing, with the weight of trout caught here averaging 2lb 5oz (1.2kg).

VALLEY VILLAGES

Chew Valley boasts many picturesque villages, the closest being Chew Stoke, with its delightful, red sandstone church, pond and unusual rectory. In the 18th century the village was famous for its bell-foundry.

Neighbouring Chew Magna is particularly pretty with its neat rows of whitewashed, terraced cottages and Georgian houses. The parish church (a Grade One Listed building) has a peal of eight bells, cast at Chew Stoke, which play a hymn tune every four hours. (See also page 29.)

Nearby Stanton Drew is famous for its Three Stone Circles and the Cove – three massive stones, believed to have been an ancient ritual centre. Legends abound as to their origin; the best known is that they represent a wedding party turned to stone for daring to dance on a Sunday.

The Lake seen from the summit of Knowle Hill

FURTHER AFIELD

Chew Valley Lake is situated within easy reach of the cathedral city of Wells (see page 86), and of Bath (see pages 8–12), with its excellent shops and Roman baths. The Mendip Hills south of the lake (see pages 64–5) offer many scenic walks and drives, notably at Ebbor Gorge and Cheddar (see page 28). A visit to Cheddar provides an opportunity to expore the famous caves, and the hills above Ebbor Gorge give views over the Somerset Levels.

CHARTERHOUSE
Somerset. Hamlet off B3371, 3 miles (5km) NE of Cheddar

▷ Charterhouse is stiuated on top of the Mendips, where the Romans mined lead. A small Roman amphitheatre survives. Mining continued from medieval times until 1885.

(See also Feature: The Mendip Hills, pages 64–5.)

CHEDDAR
Somerset. Town on A371, 8 miles (13km) NW of Wells

▷ Cheddar is famous for its deep limestone gorge and the caves below. There are cliffs of 400ft (120m) either side of the gorge, with the road at the bottom. The 274 steps of Jacob's Ladder lead to the upper level from the village. The caves are large, with stalagmites and other formations, and there is evidence of occupation in palaeolithic times. The widflower known as the Cheddar pink grows only here, and the famous cheese was named after the area.

(See also Feature: The Mendip Hills, pages 64–5.)

Cheddar Showcaves & Gorge
On B3135
Tel: 01934 742343

▷ Cheddar boasts Britain's two most beautifully illuminated showcaves – spectacular Gough's Cave and Cox's Cave with its stunning colours – plus 'The Crystal Quest', a dark walk fantasy adventure underground. The 'Cheddar Man' exhibition includes Britain's oldest complete skeleton, which experts believe to be 9,000 years old. You can climb Jacob's Ladder to Pavey's Lookout Tower and Gorge Walk, and the daring can pre-book an Adventure Caving Expedition (the minimum for the caving expedition is 12).

Open all year, daily. Closed Xmas.

Dramatic effects of light and shade in Cheddar Gorge

'It is a praty clothing town, and hath a faire church,' wrote John Leland, reporting on Chew Magna to Henry VIII in 1545. It is still a pretty village today, but any air of prosperity probably has more to do with its proximity to Bristol than with the cloth trade. The church, partly Norman, is, as so often, the strongest link with the wool era. It is memorable chiefly for the 15th-century tower and its fearsome gang of gargoyles. Inside is a large rood screen, and a wooden tomb effigy over which hangs an air of mystery. It claims to be Sir John de Hauteville, and he lies, rather uncomfortably, on his side, propped up on one elbow, legs crossed, one foot resting on an upright lion. He wears 14th-century armour, but other details do not tie in with the date. Near the church is a striking 16th-century building known either as the Old Schoolroom (for that it is what is was from 1842 to 1894) or the Church Alehouse, one-time venue for parish parties. Chew Court, once part of the Bishop of Bath and Wells' Palace of Chew, has an imposing gateway, above which is the old courtroom. The High Street is flanked by unusual raised pavements, some good Georgian houses and pleasant cottages.

CHEW MAGNA
SOMERSET. VILLAGE ON B3130, 6 MILES (10KM) S OF BRISTOL

Chew Stoke is a sizeable village, close to Chew Valley Lake, with a reservoir created in 1956 to provide water for Bristol and now used for sailing and fishing as well.
(See also Picnic site: Chew Valley Lake, pages 26–27.)

CHEW STOKE
SOMERSET. VILLAGE OFF B3114, 7 MILES (11KM) S OF BRISTOL

A town since Saxon times, Chippenham is now large and bustling. The old centre is tucked into a loop of the River Avon, with the best parts around the church (with an unusual imitation medieval spire and tower of 1633). The Old Yelde Hall, formerly the town hall, is 16th-century timber-framed, and now houses the museum. Maud Heath left money in 1474 for a causeway from Wick Hill, and there is a statue of her which dates from 1838. Chippenham has several other timber-framed buildings, and Georgian houses.

CHIPPENHAM
WILTSHIRE. TOWN ON A4, 12 MILES (19KM) NE OF BATH

The wide main street is lined with stone buildings, ranging from the 16th to the 20th century, all in scale with each other. The 'Chipping' part of the name means 'market', which was held in the broad street. There is a large early 16th-century church tower.

CHIPPING SODBURY
GLOUCESTERSHIRE. TOWN ON A432, 11 MILES (18KM) NE OF BRISTOL

Britain's second largest Roman town, strategically placed at the crossing of the Fosse Way and Ermin Way, became the site of a large Saxon Abbey, prospered as a centre of the medieval wool trade and went on to become an important market town. Some of this history is still visible in the Roman amphitheatre and other buildings, including the Norman abbey gatehouse, the remains of the 13th-century

CIRENCESTER
GLOUCESTERSHIRE. TOWN OFF A419, 14 MILES (18KM) NW OF SWINDON

Market Square, Cirencester

St John's Hospital, the Weavers' Hall of the 1340s and the old grammar school of 1464, as well as an array of houses of the 17th and 18th centuries.

St John's is one of the finest 'wool' churches of the Cotswolds, mainly 15th-century, with a tall tower, a huge and highly embellished south porch (which was used for many years as a town hall), several 16th-century chapels and an exceptional array of medieval brasses and later monuments.

Cirencester's Roman story is told at the Corinium museum (see below). The vast and magnificent Cirencester Park was established outside the town by Lord Bathurst at the turn of the 17th century.

Corinium Museum
PARK ST
TEL: 01285 655611

The full-scale reconstructions used in the Corinium Museum displays vividly evoke the way people lived during Roman times. Special exhibitions are held throughout the year. There is a Cotswold Prehistory gallery, and galleries on Roman military history, the Roman town of Corinium and the Civil War in the Cotswolds.

Open all year, certain days. Closed Xmas.

CLEVEDON
SOMERSET. TOWN ON B3124,
8 MILES (13KM) NE OF
WESTON-SUPER-MARE

Clevedon was extremely popular as a resort in Regency and early Victorian times, but later it was overtaken by Weston-Super-Mare (see page 88) because Clevedon was not on the railway. There are still many villas, a large church of 1839 and a long but simple iron pier of 1868. Inland lies Clevedon Court (see page 31) an interesting

medieval manor house with a 12th-century tower, 13th-century hall and 18th-century terraced garden.

▶ This is a remarkably complete 14th-century house, and one of the oldest of its type to have survived anywhere in Britain. Incorporated into it is an even older tower which had been built as a defence against marauding Welsh from across the Bristol Channel. Later additions and modifications have not detracted form the charm of Clevedon Court. The focal point of the medieval manor house was the Great Hall, which was divided by a screen passage. One side was the buttery and kitchen, on the other the main body of the hall, used as the general living area of the household. Beyond that were the living quarters of the lord of the manor and his family. Clevedon Court also retains its early 14th-century chapel, situated on the first floor, which has beautiful and intricate tracery.

In the 18th and 19th centuries Clevedon became a meeting place for the avant-garde of the day. One owner during the late Victorian era was Sir Edmund Elton, a celebrated potter, and some of his work is on display in the old kitchen of the house.

Open Etr–Sep on selected days.

Clevedon Court
SOMERSET. 1½ MILES (2.5KM)
EAST OF CLEVEDON
TEL: 01275 872257

Clevedon Court

▶ This large village across the Congresbury Yeo was a small port until 1900 and supposedly founded by St Congar, from whose walking stick the ancient yew in the churchyard is said to have grown. The church is mostly 15th-century outside and 13th-century inside. To the north is an Iron-Age hillfort usually known as Cadbury-Congresbury.

CONGRESBURY
SOMERSET. VILLAGE ON A370,
5 MILES (8KM) S OF CLEVEDON

Grid ref: SP103077

INFORMATION

The walk is 3¾ miles (6km) long. The terrain is gently undulating, but with muddy patches in wet conditions and one section overgrown with nettles in summer. The only road walking is through the villages

Dogs must be kept on leads. Several stiles and gates.

Pubs and café at Bibury, ice cream at the Trout Farm, refreshment van regularly at Arlington Mill.

Picnics in the dry valley below Ablington Downs

START

Ablington is a mile (1.5km) west of the A433 at Bibury. Park safely and considerately in the village,

The near-perfect harmony of the Cotswold villages within their landscape present a quintessentially English rural scene. Though the walk starts little more than a mile from the tourist rendezvous of Bibury, walkers will find peace and beauty all around.

then commence the walk at the old mill on the east side of the Coln bridge. Alternative parking is available at Swains Bridge at Coln Rogers.

DIRECTIONS

Follow the lane leading north-west beside attractive gardens overlooking the mill-stream;

beyond a gate the track proceeds past kennels, swinging up round a walled enclosure. The track descends to a gate then runs directly across the side valley, rising to a gate. With a drystone

The River Coln, viewed from Swains Bridge at Coln Rogers

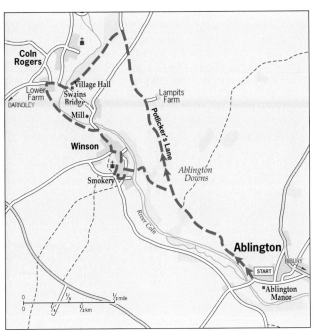

poplar grove, passing up through the larch plantation to a gate. Do not go through the gate, but bear right between conifers and fence to reach a gate/stile. Ascend the pasture, crossing to the far corner to a gate to rejoin the outward route at the Ablington Downs dry valley.

Cotswold Villages

Ablington (see page 5) has several classic Cotswold houses of which Ablington House, dating from 1650, must be pre-eminent. Its high pitched gables stand proudly behind a high drystone wall; the 19th-century stone lions came from the Houses of Parliament. Coln Rogers church, though not directly en route, is well worth a visit. It is almost unique in the Cotswolds in that is has a largely intact Saxon chancel and nave and a secluded, almost farmyard, setting. Winson is a compact village centred upon a small green which is dominated by the Georgian manor and the Saxon/Norman parish church. Notice the table tombs and old schoolhouse in the churchyard.

wall to the right, advance to a gate and enter Potlicker's Lane. From Lampits Farm this green track carries regular traffic. Meeting the minor road go forward finding a narrow path leading left by the grove and down into the valley. At the foot of the lane, beside the Village Hall, go right, crossing the broad Swains Bridge. At the road fork bear left, towards Lower Farm (Stratford Place Stud) and turn left, crossing the open gravel yard to the steps to the right of the barn. Pass along the bank above a drystone wall to a stile in the curve of the paddock fencing, proceed downwards via a gate and cross the low fence stile. Passing through the old hedge line, keep right upon the bank (ignore track gate beside Winson Mill) and continue above the mill

to a gate, joining the road directly into Winson to your right. Go left at the road junction to the triangular green. Keep right, past the church, then left by the Coln Valley Fish and Game Company (the 'Smokery'), descending the narrow lane bearing left to find a white wicket gate on your right and concrete footpath marker. Cross the paddock to a second wicket gate, then cross the stile footbridge and go through the

WHAT TO LOOK OUT FOR

In the intriguingly named Potlicker's Lane you can judge the age of the hedgerow by the variety of woody species of tree, thorn and shrub that flourish within it. During the drive from Bibury notice the quaint signpost at the first junctions in Ablington 'Bibury 4/3'.

CORSHAM

WILTSHIRE. TOWN OFF A4, 4 MILES (6KM) SW OF CHIPPENHAM

▶ This must be the most picturesque town in Wiltshire, with the centre full of stone houses, many of them 17th-century and gabled. There are also stone Georgian houses, a town hall of 1784, and the Hungerford almshouses, dating from 1668 with a very pretty porch. Corsham Court (in the town) is Elizabethan and Victorian imitation Elizabethan, with fine paintings and furniture and park and gardens, partly laid out by 'Capability' Brown and Humphry Repton. The Underground Quarry Centre is a Bath stone quarry.

CRICKLADE

WILTSHIRE. VILLAGE OFF A419, 7 MILES (11KM) NW OF SWINDON

The village of Cricklade

▶ This Saxon town still has the square earthen defences built in Alfred's time. There is a church with a very prominent 16th-century tower, and another little Norman one tucked into the High Street. Seventeenth-century and Georgian stone and stucco houses are mixed with modern. Robert Jenner's school dating from 1651 is of graceful design, and a meadow to the north has thousands of fritillaries in May.

CROFTON PUMPING STATION

CROFTON, WILTSHIRE. 6 MILES (9.6KM) SE OF MARLBOROUGH, SIGNPOSTED FROM A338/A346/B3087 AT BURBAGE

TEL: 01672 870300

▶ The oldest working beam engine in the world still in its original building and still doing its original job, the Boulton and Watt 1812, is to be found in this rural spot. Its companion is a Harvey's of Hayle dating from 1845. Both are steam driven, from a coal-fired boiler, and pump water into the summit level of the Kennet and Avon Canal with a lift of 40 feet (12m). Pleasant country walks can be taken along the canal towpath and to a working windmill near by.

Open Apr–Oct, daily. Steaming certain weekends.

Just north of Lydney lies the headquarters of the Dean Forest Railway where a number of steam locomotives, as well as coaches, wagons and railway equipment are on show. Waggon-ways built to transport minerals out of the forest in the 18th century were later converted to railways, and the Dean Forest Railway is one of them; it began as a horse-drawn tramway built by the Severn and Wye Railway, and was gradually converted to steam traction and railway standards.

Guided tours are available by arrangement. There is also a gift shop, museum, riverside walk and forest trail. Special events are arranged throughout the year.

Open all year, daily. Steam days: Sun from Etr–Sep, Wed Jun–Aug. Santa special, Dec.

DEAN FOREST RAILWAY
LYDNEY, GLOUCESTERSHIRE
NORCHARD CENTRE, NEW
MILLS, FOREST RD. 1 MILE
(1.5KM) N AT NEW MILLS ON
B4234, WELL SIGNPOSTED
FROM A48 TEL: 01594
845840 & 843423
(RECORDED INFORMATION)

Devizes is a true country town, with some early cottages and many handsome Georgian buildings. The market place is especially good, with a fancy market cross of 1814. The medieval castle has been replaced by a more elaborate Victorian one, with a big gatehouse. There is a classical town hall of 1806, and many inns, because Devizes was a coaching stop. The Kennet and Avon Canal has a famous flight of 29 locks in only 2 miles (3km) to the west of the town; there is a canal museum too. Devizes Museum includes archaeology, art and natural history.

DEVIZES
WILTSHIRE. TOWN ON A342,
10 MILES (16KM) SE OF
CHIPPENHAM

This museum houses world-famous collections from the Neolithic, Bronze and Iron Age; there is a Bronze Age gallery, an art gallery with a John Piper window, displays of natural history, and a Wiltshire research library.

Open all year, Mon–Sat. Closed BHs.

Devizes Museum
41 LONG ST
TEL: 01380 727369

This quartet of attractive settlements (Abbots, Leer, Middle, Rouse) is strung along Dunt Brook. Leer and Middle are quiet farm hamlets. Rouse has an unusual Saxon and Norman church on a steep hillside with an interior rich in history. The road at Abbots (see below) is partly submerged beneath the brook, and St Peter's Church has a notable Norman font and ancient ironmongery on its door.

DUNTISBOURNES, THE
GLOUCESTERSHIRE. VILLAGES
AND HAMLETS OFF A417,
5 MILES (8KM) NW OF
CIRENCESTER

Duntisbourne Abbots is the most northerly of the group of four Duntisbournes. As picturesque as many other Cotswold villages, they also have strong associations with the followers of William Morris, who first popularised the Cotswolds. In the parish of Duntisbourne Rouse, to the south-west of the village, lies Pinbury Park, where Ernest Gimson, brilliant interpreter of the Arts and Crafts movement, and his fellow designer-craftsmen, the Barnsley brothers, came to live at the

DUNTISBOURNE ABBOTS
GLOUCESTERSHIRE
6 MILES (9.5KM) NW OF
CIRENCESTER

beginning of the century. Cotswold Farm, near Duntisbourne Abbots, was enlarged by Sidney Barnsley in 1926 and has a window by Edward Burne-Jones. In medieval time Duntisbourne Abbots, as indicated by its name, belonged to the Abbot of Gloucester. His mainly Norman but much-restored church is approached through a lych-gate, past some good table tombs. Better known is the small church at Duntisbourne Rouse, which has Saxon origins. Making use of the slope on which it stands, the Normans built a crypt under the chancel. The little tower has a saddleback roof and the medieval misericords are to be relished. Duntisbourne Leer, one of several places in the valley where the River Church has to be forded, and Middle Duntisbourne complete this beautifully situated quartet of mellow Cotswold villages (see page 35).

DYRHAM

GLOUCESTERSHIRE. HAMLET OFF A46, 4 MILES (6KM) S OF CHIPPING SODBURY

▶ This small Cotswold village is perhaps best known for Dyrham Park (National Trust), a handsome late 17th-century mansion, still with many interiors of that date; the ancient deer park still has its herd of fallow deer. (See below.)

Dyrham Park
TEL: 0117 937 2501

▶ There was once a Tudor house on this site, but the Dyrham Park we see today, built for William Blathwayt, is entirely a creation of the William and Mary period. Blathwayt rose from fairly modest beginnings through the Civil Service to hold a number of top government jobs and found favour with William III both for his administrative abilities and because he spoke Dutch. Blathwayt also made an advantageous marriage to the heiress of the Dyrham estate, but it was not until after the death of both his in-laws and his wife that he began to replace their family home.

The mansion was constructed in two stages, first in 1692 by an unknown Huguenot architect, and around the turn of the century by one of the foremost architects of the day, William Talman.

Between them they created a splendid house, the design of which displays unusual restraint for the times.

Dyrham Park has changed little over the years and all the furniture, paintings and pottery we see in the house today were collected by Blathwayt himself. The series of apartments are decorated and furnished very much with a Dutch influence, including paintings of the Dutch school and a collection of blue-and-white Delft ware; there are Dutch-style gardens, too.

Open Etr–Oct, certain days

Most preserved railways are the result of a shared vision which drives widely different people to pool their skills. The East Somerset Railway, however, was the brainchild of just one man – and he holds elephants responsible. In 1967 the wildlife painter David Shepherd had just sold all his paintings of elephants on exhibition in New York when the opportunity arose to indulge in his other passion – steam railways – by buying one of British Rail's last steam locomotives. Naturally he needed somewhere to keep it, along with the other locomotives he was later to acquire, and this 2-mile (3-km) line is the result of a long search.

EAST SOMERSET RAILWAY
CRANMORE, 2½ MILES (4KM)
E OF SHEPTON MALLET
TEL: 01749 880417

The mansion house at Dyrham in its parkland setting

The railway has a strong environmental theme, which is immediately apparent to visitors: a wildlife information centre adjoins the car park, and beside the station is a British-built engine which saw service in Zambia and was presented to David Shepherd by President Kaunda in recognition of his work on behalf of African wildlife. The lush pasture and woods through which the line passes are home to badgers, foxes and deer, and the deep Doulting Cutting abounds with ancient fossils, for which it has been designated a Site of Special Scientific Interest.

The 12-minute journey can be broken at the halt provided for picnickers at Merryfield Lane on the outward journey, or at Cranmore West on the return. The halt here enables you to walk through the marvellous replica of a Great Western Railway engine shed and admire the well-equipped workshops from a viewing platform. Here the East Somerset's eight steam locomotives are overhauled. They range from the huge frieght locomotive, *Black Prince*, to the tiny industrial tanks, *Lord Fisher* and *Lady Nan*, and include a rare crane tank from a steelworks in Staffordshire.

Train service: early Mar–end Nov on selected days.
Also Santa specials, Dec.

FRAMPTON ON SEVERN

Gloucestershire. Village off A38, 7 miles (11km) W of Stroud

One of the prerequisites of a perfect village is a green, but few can rival Frampton's. Its 22 acres (9ha), divided by the road that runs through the village, make it one of England's largest, and three ponds and a cricket pitch lie within it. Known as Rosamund's Green, it lends added dignity to the half-timbered and Georgian houses that line its sides. Henry II's mistress, 'Fair Rosamund', Jane Clifford, is said to have been born here. Kept by Henry in a house in Woodstock surrounded by a maze, she is reputed to have been poisoned by Henry's Queen Eleanor, who found her way through the maze by following a thread of the king's cloak. The seat of the Clifford family is Frampton Court, built in the 1730s in Vanbrugh style, probably by John Strachan of Bristol. In the 1980s a beautiful collection of Victorian flower paintings, done by lady members of the family, was discovered in an attic and published as *The Frampton Flora*. Visible from the road is William Halfpenny's 'Strawberry Hill' Gothic orangery, with pretty ogee windows. In front of it, but not visible from the green, is a rectangular canal.On the other side of the green is the family's 15th-century, partly half-timbered manor house. Further down the green the houses are smaller and less spaced out, but none the less attractive, some gabled and thatched. Eventually the road bends away from the green to wind through the rest of the village, finally reaching the church, which is set apart from the village beside the Sharpness Canal. The canal-keeper's Doric-style house is not far away and boats pass within yards of the

Gazetteer

church. It dates mainly from the 14th century, with some 15th-century additions, and with most of its windows being of clear glass it is pleasantly light and airy. There are some notable monuments, particularly the tablet made by John Pearce, 'statuary and diagraphist', in memory of his brothers.

This large town is noted for its handsome Georgian stone houses and cottages densely packed in steep streets. Cloth-making made the town rich from medieval times to 1800, with a decline thereafter. The best buildings are the big 1707 classical Congregational chapel and the Blue House of 1726. The railway station (1850) is all wood – a rare survivor. There is a local museum. (See also page 70.)

FROME
*SOMERSET. TOWN OFF A362,
11 MILES (18KM) S OF BATH*

Glastonbury is a good-looking small market town, full of handsome stone buildings. Many were part of the abbey, including the Tribunal (English Heritage), the 15th-century abbey courthouse (now with a museum on the Iron-Age lake villages, see Westhay) and the George and Pilgrims hotel; the 16th-century Church of St John is the main town church. There is a pretty market cross of 1846 in the centre, and several 'New Age' shops.

GLASTONBURY
*SOMERSET. TOWN ON A39,
5 MILES (9KM) S OF WELLS*

The ruins of Glastonbury Abbey

The abbey ruins (see below) spread over a large area and include the famous octagonal abbot's kitchen (14th century) and the Holy Thorn Museum. The 14th-century tithe barn is now the Somerset Museum of Rural Life, with displays on life in the county. The Chalice Well was the centre of an 18th-century spa. Glastonbury Tor, 521 feet (158m) high, is prominent from miles around, and is topped by the tower of a ruined church. The Somerset Levels extend towards the north.

Tradition maintains that the impressive, medieval abbey ruins stand at the birthplace of Christianity in Britain. This is where Joseph of Arimathea is said to have brought the Holy Grail and to have founded a chapel in AD 61, planting his staff in the ground where it flowered both at Christmas and Easter. Later, it is said, King Arthur and Guinevere were buried at Glastonbury; and the abbey was a place of pilgrimage in the Middle Ages. The present abbey ruins date from after a fire in 1184, and are mostly of the 12th and 13th centuries. The abbey fell into decay after the Dissolution.

Open all year, daily. Closed Xmas.

Glastonbury Abbey
*MAGDALENE ST. ON A361
BETWEEN FROME & TAUNTON
TEL: 01458 832267*

INFORMATION

Total Distance
18 miles (29km)

Difficulty
Easy

OS Map
Landranger 1:50,000 sheet 183
(Yeovil & Frome)

Tourist Information
Glastonbury, tel: 01458
832954; Wells, tel: 01749
672552

Nearest railway station
Somerton (3 miles/5km)

Cycle shops/hire
Bikes 'n' Bits, Wells, tel: 01749
670260; City Cycles, Wells, tel:
01749 675096; Pedallers,
Glastonbury, tel: 01458
831117; Street Cycle Co, Street,
tel: 01458 447882

Refreshments
Numerous tea shops, cafés and
pubs in Glastonbury, plus the
Barton Inn at Barton St David and
the Rose and Portcullis, Butleigh
which caters for families. Also the
Baltonsburgh Village Stores.

START
The historic market town of
Glastonbury is located on the
A39, 6 miles (9km) south of
Wells. There is plenty of
reasonably-priced parking in the
town centre (pay-and-display).

This gentle, 3–4 hour route is almost traffic-free, with plenty of opportunity for picnicking and enjoying the scenery and wildlife havens. Mainly flat or with gentle climbs, there is a short steep climb back into Glastonbury, but this can be walked easily. The area can become busy on bank holidays and fine weekends. Some lanes are quite narrow, so take care with small children when riding alongside the river or canal.

DIRECTIONS

1. From Glastonbury, head up the
High Street and turn right at the
T-junction at the top to join the
A361, following signs for
'Shepton Mallet'. Continue ahead
for a few hundred yards to the
mini-roundabout, then bear left,
keeping on the A361. This road
can be busy at times, so take
care. Almost opposite is the
fascinating Museum of Rural Life.

2. After 875 yards (800m) just
beyond Well House Lane
(leading to Glastonbury Tor) turn
right into Cinnamon Lane. Take
great care; this lane drops steeply
and there can be loose gravel
around. At the bottom, follow the
tight left-hand bend, then enjoy
the traffic-free lane. Take the first
right and follow the canal for

1 mile (1.5km), when the road
leaves the canal-side; continue for
about another mile (1.5km).

3. At the end, turn left by the past
box, then right, following the sign
for 'West Bradley'. To visit the
West Pennard Court Barn, turn left
here and continue for ¼ mile
(0.5km) to find the barn on your
right. Retrace your tracks to rejoin
the main route. After 100 yards
(91m) turn right again, still
signposted 'West Bradley'.
Follow the signs and the run of the
road, heading for Parbrook.
Swing round the bend at West
Bradley House Fruit Farm, ease
up the rise past the parish church,
then turn right towards the
charming villages of Hornblotton
and Lydford.

4. Pass the Old School and climb the rise, turning right at the farm at the top, signed 'Baltonsborough and Glastonbury'. Enjoy the easy roll along to Baltonsborough. Go straight past the phone box and down the hill to the junction. The Greyhound pub offers a welcome break, and 100 yards (91m) down the road opposite is the village store. Turn left towards Barton St David and follow the well-surfaced lane alongside the river for a while before moving over the river on a tight hump-backed bridge to enter Barton St David.

5. At the 'major' crossroads (with the phone box opposite) turn right towards Butleigh. Pass the Barton Inn (the converted church), then

continue out of the village. Drop down into Butleigh before tackling the ascent through the village to The Rose and Portcullis Inn.

6. Suitably refreshed, turn right into Sub Road towards Glastonbury. Go past Butleigh Court, then continue for 1½ miles (2.5km) through Butleigh Wootton before turning right at the top of a rise, down across the levels back towards Glastonbury Cross Cow Bridge. Go through the '30' signs, and take the first right into Old Butleigh Road, up the steep ascent. Turn right at the top then, after 220 yards (200m), turn left at the mini-roundabout through the traffic-calming scheme then left again back into Glastonbury High Street to the start point.

Mysterious Glastonbury Tor

PLACES OF INTEREST

Glastonbury

This town abounds in places of interest and also in mystery and legend. Particularly noteworthy are the Abbey and grounds (see also page 39) and the Museum of Rural Life near by. Glastonbury sits on the ancient Isle of Avalon, long associated with Joseph of Arimathea, and with King Arthur and his knights. The legend of Joseph says that as he leaned on his staff here it took root and flowered, a sign which he took to mean he should build a church. The chapel which he founded in AD 61 was the forerunner of Glastonbury Abbey.

WHAT TO LOOK OUT FOR

This route features a wide variety of hedgerow birdlife, as well as opportunities to see kingfishers and heron. There are many old houses, and also some tasteful conversions of barns and churches. Butleigh Court comes as a complete surprise, its castellated features contrastingly starkly with other buildings en route. Note also the variety of farming styles, with arable, sheep and dairy farms all within a very small area. Glastonbury Tor is a famous landmark.

Glastonbury Tor

Visible from most of this route, the mound supports the only remains of St Michael's Church – the Chalice Well at the foot of the Tor is supposedly the resting place of the Holy Grail.

Wells

Some 6 miles (10km) away is an interesting city famed for its large cathedral, whose Green makes an ideal picnic site. Other attractions here include the Bishop's Palace, Vicar's Close, a street inhabited continuously since the early 1500s, the Wells Cathedral School and the city's regular Wednesday and Saturday markets. (See also page 86.)

Street

The main attraction of this town is the 'Clark's Village', a well-designed purpose-built complex of shops selling high-quality 'seconds' and featuring a variety

The west front of Wells Cathedral

▶ There seems no limit to the achievements — and ambitions — of railway preservationists. The Gloucestershire Warwickshire Railway (the other GWR) started with nothing more than a trackless railway route, with few surviving buildings between Broadway and Cheltenham Racecourse. It has already re-opened 6 miles (9.5km) of the line, and its ultimate goal is to buy further freeholds to enable it to run all the way to Stratford-upon-Avon, where the line originally met the surviving commuter route to Birmingham. To rebuild the existing line between the headquarters at Toddington and Far Stanley, volunteers have had to rebuild platforms, dismantle all manner of buildings and artefacts for re-erection and set up facilities for the repair and maintenance of locomotives and carriages — none of the stations on the route even had an engine shed.

Before leaving on the 50-minute return journey, passengers can visit Toddington station's added attraction of the 2-foot (610-mm) gauge North Gloucestershire Railway — which offers rides behind a German engine; others from Natal and Poland can be seen under restoration.

The railway runs south from Toddington through the picturesque Vale of Evesham, awash with apple and fruit blossom in spring. The produce of the orchards was once a major source of traffic for the railway, which was closed by British Rail in 1977. Running parallel with the line to the east is the Cotswold escarpment, its limestone providing the lovely honey-coloured stone that is used for many of the district's buildings.

In the lea of the ridge are the remains of the 13th-century Hailes Abbey, once served by a halt on the railway. Beyond the hamlet of Didbrook the observant eye can discern remnants of the medieval strip farming system, denoted by long rectangles of raised ground. Another charming sight is provided by the goats which are used to keep down the grass on embankments and cuttings — infinitely preferable to spraying with chemicals.

Winchcombe station building stood at Monmouth (Troy) until it was dismantled and each stone numbered to assist re-erection. As the train pulls away from this popular Cotswold town, it enters a cutting leading to Greet Tunnel, at 693 yards (633m) the second longest on a preserved railway. The line stops in the middle of the country, pending extension, but the short wait while the locomotive runs round is no hardship in such surroundings.

Train service: steam weekends from Apr–Sept, Sundays only to early October; also diesel selected days. Santa specials, Dec.

GLOUCESTERSHIRE WARWICKSHIRE RAILWAY
TODDINGTON, 7 MILES (11KM)
NE OF CHELTENHAM
TEL: 01242 621405

GREAT BEDWYN

WILTSHIRE. VILLAGE OFF A4, 5 MILES (8KM) SW OF HUNGERFORD

▶ Great Bedwyn today is a village, but in medieval times it was a town, and has a large 12th- to 13th-century church. Mason's Yard is decorated all over with stone carvings and houses the Bedwyn Stone Museum (see below).

Bedwyn Stone Museum
TEL: 01672 870043

▶ This small but special open-air museum explains the ancient secrets of the stonemason, showing how carvings have a language of their own. A fine sequence of carvings can be seen in the nearby church.

Open all year, daily.

GREAT WITCOMBE ROMAN VILLA

GLOUCESTERSHIRE. OFF A417, ½ MILE (1KM) S OF RESERVOIR IN WITCOMBE PARK
TEL: 0117 9750700

▶ The remains found at Great Witcombe are of a large Roman Villa built around three sides of a courtyard. Several mosaic pavements have been preserved and there is also evidence of a hypocaust (a system of underfloor heating developed by the Romans).

Open at any reasonable time. Please telephone for details of guided tours.

Hamptworth Lodge could be said to be a monument to the Arts and Crafts movement of the Edwardian era, despite having the appearance of a Jacobean house. It was actually built in 1912, possibly to the design of the original 1620s house.

Harold Moffatt, who commissioned the new house, was a keen follower of the movement and only traditional building methods were used in its construction, under the direction of architect Guy Dawber – often called 'the Lutyens of the west'. The brickwork designs are particularly notable, and a feature has been made of the rainwater furniture and the diamond-cut inscriptions on some of the leaded windows. The Great Hall is of baronial proportions and has an organ gallery, complete with a huge Willis organ.

The multi-talented Moffatt even went so far as to make much of the furniture himself, and these pieces are also an accurate representation of Jacobean style. There is genuine 17th-century furniture here too, as well as a fine collection of old clocks. The wall coverings are particularly interesting; a variety of woods were used for the panelling, and one room is lined with leather.

Harold Moffatt was a man who was energetically true to his ideals and remains an inspiration to the present owner of the house.

Open daily, except Sunday; closed Oct–Apr.

HAMPTWORTH LODGE
Wiltshire
Landford, 9 miles (14.5km)
SE of Salisbury
Tel: 01794 390215

The medieval church in Haresfield is well worth a visit, as is the climb to Haresfield Beacon on the Cotswold Edge for spectacular views across the Severn Vale.

(See also Walk: Haresfield Beacon, pages 46–7.)

HARESFIELD
Gloucestershire. Village off
B4008, 4 miles (6km) NW
of Stroud

Heale House and its eight acres (3ha) of beautiful gardens lie beside the River Avon at Middle Woodford. Much of the house is unchanged since King Charles II sheltered here after the battle of Worcester in 1651. The garden provides a wonderfully varied collection of plants, shrubs, and musk and other roses, growing in the formal setting of clipped hedges and mellow stonework, which are at their best in June and July. In January great drifts of snowdrops and aconites bring early colour and a promise of spring.

Particularly lovely in spring and autumn is the water garden, planted with magnificent magnolia and acers, surrounding the authentic Japanese Tea House and Nikko Bridge which makes an exciting focus in this part of the garden. National Gardens Day is held here on the first Sunday in August, and there is also a specialist plant centre.

Open all year, daily.

HEALE GARDENS
Middle Woodford,
Wiltshire. 4 miles (6.5km)
N of Salisbury, between
A360 & A345
Tel: 01722 782504

This walk takes in two contrasting spurs of the Cotswold escarpment – the open aspect of the Shortwood spar, overlooking Standish Woods, and the narrow, steep Haresfield Beacon, almost craggy by comparison, offering views across the Severn valley towards the Forest of Dean.

Grid ref: SO832086

INFORMATION

The walk is 2 miles (3km) long, three with optional extension.
Firm paths, with one brief, but steep ascent on to Haresfield Beacon.
A few stiles. No road walking.
Dogs must be on a lead.
Pub (Edgemoor Inn) on Cotswold Way, ¼ mile (0.5km) south of Edge on the A4173.
Picnic places on grassy Shortwood spur.

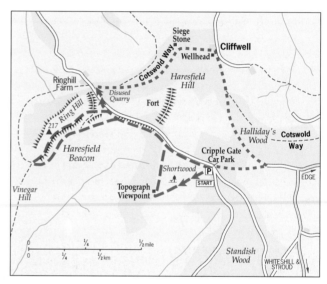

START

The Cripple Gate National Trust car park is situated 2 miles (3km) north of Stroud, accessible from the A4173 Gloucester road at Edge. From here travel south following the signs for Haresfield Beacon.

DIRECTIONS

From the squeeze-stile, beside the National Trust information panel in the car park, follow the track south-west to the Topograph Viewpoint. Take the track due north and just before reaching the wall, turn left down a woodland track parallel to the road. At the foot of the incline cross a stile. Continue for about 20 yards (18m) and fork left, following the wall/fence round and up to a stile. Keep to the wall at the foot of the steep Haresfield Beacon bank for about ½ mile (1km). Eventually the path turns to the right and where you see a stile on the left, take the path slanting sharply right on to the tip of the ridge. A grass path climbs the ridge steadily through the light thorn scrub, ascending quite steeply to the beacon site and trig point via rampart ditches. Follow the southern rampart of the hill fort eastward to a stile. Join the fenced path beside a field (good views). Where the principal promontory fort ditch cuts across the neck of the ridge the path encounters a hunting-gate and wall squeeze-stile, then winds down through more broken ground to the road.

To extend the walk turn left at the collection box, following the road as far as Ringhill Farm. At the farm turn right following 'Cotswold Way' signs. Continue along the path, passing the Siege Stone, dated 1643, commemorating the siege of

Walk

WHAT TO LOOK OUT FOR

There is much wildlife in the old scarpland, grassland and beechwood. Notable birds include wood warblers and spotted flycatchers in the woods, while skylarks prefer more open terrain. The occasional buzzard may be seen wheeling high overhead. Be sure to look out for butterflies and wild orchids.

Gloucester. On reaching the road and wellhead, turn right and continue along the road for about ½ mile (1km). Turn right at the sign for Haresfield Beacon and return to the car park.

For the main walk bear immediately right down the steps next to the National Trust collection box, signposted 'Cotswold Way'; this path slants left and shortly rejoins the outward path, rising to the stile. Ascend the incline, maintaining course at the top and walking parallel to the wall over the Shortwood pasture to reach the car park.

Shortwood Topograph

This unusual relief plinth stands in the midst of three Cotswold escarpments of precious

unimproved calcareous grassland and beech woodland. The view extends over Standish Woods, the twin towers of the decommissioned Berkeley Nuclear Power Station, three loops of the Severn, the Forest of Dean and the Black Mountains.

Haresfield Beacon

At the 50-mile (80-km) mid-point of the Cotswold Way between Chipping Camden and Bath, the Beacon is surmounted by Ring Hill camp and the old Ordnance Survey triangulation station, made obsolete now by satellite mapping. The narrow ridge bears the scars of many centuries of surface quarrying.

The edge of Haresfield Beacon

*H*at Gate is located in the heart of the rolling chalk downs of Wiltshire, less than 3 miles (5km) outside Marlborough, on the edge of Savernake Forest with its ancient trees and majestic avenue of beeches. The picnic site is especially suitable for families.

HOW TO GET THERE

Take the A346 from Marlborough to Burbage, and head south for about 3 miles (5km). Turn right at the junction marked for Wootton Rivers, and the clearly signposted entrance to Hat Gate is immediately to your left. There is free parking along the roadside.

Hat Gate picnic site

FACILITIES

Spacious parkland site with numerous picnic tables.

All roads in the privately owned Savernake Forest are open to visitors until dusk.

Hat Gate is situated at the southernmost corner of the beautiful Savernake Forest (see

page 76), a massive expanse of woodland, glades and nature trails. There are plenty of picnic tables scattered about the grassy parkland, with huge trees to provide shade. The forest itself has been in the wardenship of one family since 1066, boasting royal connections with Henry VIII, who hunted here and married a local girl, Jane Seymour. It remains the only English forest in private hands. The Grand Avenue was planted by 'Capability' Brown in the 1790s.

A HISTORIC WATERWAY

At the pretty village of Wootton Rivers, stroll along the attractive towpath of the Kennet and Avon Canal, or take a boat trip to nearby Pewsey to visit the heritage centre. Further west at Crofton, visit the Crofton Pumping Station, a fascinating museum containing the world's oldest working steam-driven beam engines, built in the early 19th century to supply water to the canal. (See also page 34). From the same period, Wilton Windmill, the only operating windmill in Wiltshire, stands proudly on a chalk ridge overlooking the rolling countryside.

WHITE HORSES

The six giant white horses cut into the chalky hillsides of Wiltshire are a most unusual feature of this

region; two of them are situated in the Vale of Pewsey. The horse at Alton Barnes was cut in 1812 by a man called Jack the Painter, for £20. It is said that he took the money and disappeared before completing the work. He was eventually traced and hanged for his crime. (See also page 15).

CLOSE BY

Don't miss the extraordinary Stone Circle at Avebury; property of the National Trust, it is one of the most important megalithic monuments in Europe. Neighbouring Marlborough is certainly worth a visit; and exceptional example of a traditional country town, its wide main street is lined with Georgian Houses, attractive shops and a colourful market every Wednesday. (See also pages 5 and 60).

Crofton Pumping Station

HOLT

*WILTSHIRE. VILLAGE ON
B3107, 2 MILES (3KM) N OF
TROWBRIDGE*

The Courts

*3 MILES (5KM) SW OF
MELKSHAM
TEL: 01225 782340*

▶ This was a spa in the 18th century, based around a natural spring. Ham Green is pretty, with Georgian and earlier houses set around the green. The Courts (see below) has delightful gardens open to visitors. Close by is Great Chalfield Manor (see pages 15 and 53), a beautiful moated Tudor manor house.

(See also Cycle ride: Holt and Lacock, pages 52–3.)

▶ As the name suggest, The Courts was the building where the cloth weavers of Bradford-on-Avon, a mile (1.5km) away, brought their disputes for settlement, and indeed at one time cloth was made on the site as a cloth mill stood next to the house. In 1900 the well-known architect, Sir George Hastings, bought The Courts, introduced many of the architectural features to its gardens – including the yew and box hedges as a background for the stone ornaments – and built the conservatory. From 1921, however, it was owned by Major T C E Goff and Lady Cecilie, his wife, and it was she who, influenced by Gertrude Jekyll, laid out the series of 'garden rooms' at The Courts which offer an ever-changing series of vistas and make the visitor feel that the gardens are bigger than their 7 acres (2.8ha).

The garden is reached through an avenue of pleached limes at the front of the house. At the end of the lawn there is a fernery backed by a *Lonicera nitida* hedge. To the east of the house (which is not open to the public) is a lawn dominated by eight stone pillars that used to have chains hung between them for drying the cloth produced at the mill.

The lily pond was made by Lady Cecilie Goff, and its paved area is dominated in autumn by sumach and a purple berberis underplanted with bergenias and diascias. The pond itself boasts dark-red, pink and white waterlilies, and is surrounded by a herbaceous bed planted with lavenders, irises and roses. The borders beyond the lily pond are full of hostas, astilbes, rodgersias, and a fragrant *Viburnum carlesii*.

A path runs around the natural shape of the lower pond to re-emerge in front of a stone pavilion where there are two deep borders planted with pink-, yellow- and purple-flowering perennials, including many hemerocallis. The Venetian Gate borders, which lead on to the house lawn, are edged with lilies, red hot pokers, lychnis and echinops. At the corner of the main lawn, to the west, is a grotto made of tufa, while a path behind it is edged with clumps of Japanese sacred bamboo and angel's fishing rod. At the end of the main lawn, the sundial is surrounded by artemesias, flag irises and two clipped, weeping pears, while the blue and yellow borders are rich with geraniums, euphorbias, achilleas and Michaelmas daisies.

Garden open Apr–Oct, certain days.

Cycle ride

*T*his moderate and mostly flat route links three National Trust properties and the area covered can become busy on bank holidays and fine weekends. Some lanes are quite narrow, so take care if riding with small children.

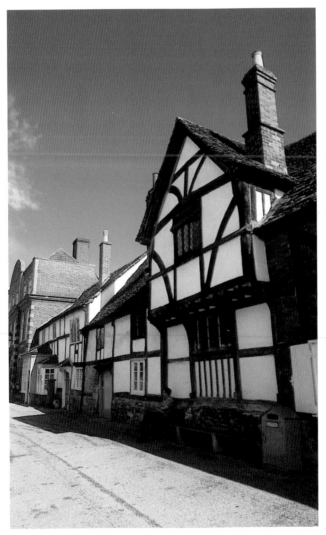

A row of attractive timbered houses at Lacock

INFORMATION

Total distance
13¼ miles (22km)

Difficulty
Moderate

OS Map
Landranger 1:50,000 sheet 173 (Swindon and Devizes)

Tourist Information
Chippenham, tel: 01249 706333: Bradford-on-Avon, tel: 01225 865797

Nearest railway stations:
Bradford-on-Avon (4 miles/ 6.5km); Trowbridge (4 miles/6.5km); Melksham (3 miles/5km)

Cycle shops/hire
Lock Inn Cottage, Bradford-on-Avon, tel: 01225 868068

Refreshments
There are many tea shops, cafés and pubs in Lacock and Bradford-on-Avon, plus the Roebuck at Westrop, the Forrester's at Atworth, the Bell at Broughton Gifford and the Harp and Crown at Gastard.

START
The National Trust village of Holt lies on the B3107 close to the River Avon. The start point is The

Courts (NT), located some 3 miles (5km) north of Trowbridge, on the B3107. (See also page 50).

DIRECTIONS

1. Leave The Courts, turning left on to the main road. After 410 yards (375m) turn right into Leigh Road opposite the Tollgate pub and enjoy the flat lane as it meanders between tall hedgerows. Shortly turn right, signed 'Holt Manor'. Ride through the grounds past the manor house and old gateway, and turn right at the end. Shortly pass Great Chalfield Manor on your left.

Follow the road sharp right through the long avenue and up the slight ascent.

2. Turn right at the junction and head down towards Broughton Gifford. After The Bell on the common, bear left, signed 'Melksham', then take the next left, signed 'Norrington Common and Shaw', into a delightful lane.

3. When you reach Shaw, turn right on to the main road and soon turn left on the B3353 heading past the church, towards Corsham. Once out of Whitley,

pass under the pylons and continue up a steady climb. Approaching Gastard, pass through the '30' signs and freewheel down the other side.

4. Just on the left-hand bend, turn right into Plains End opposite the Harp and Crown. Continue to the junction with the A350. Almost opposite is a gap in the fence. Dismount, cross the road and walk through the gap. Remount, ride to the end of the road, turn left then left again into Lacock.

The courtyard at Lacock Abbey

5. Head north out of the car park into the centre of Lacock. Go straight through the village, passing the main street on your right, down the dip and up the ascent to meet the A350 after ¼ mile (0.5km). At the junction use the cycle crossing and turn right, then left into the lane almost opposite. Continue past the houses and into open country. Follow the road over the railway bridge and left, following the lane past the Roebuck pub.

6. Take the next turn left into Ladbrook Lane towards Neston and continue over the railway bridge. At the end, go straight over into Monk's Lane. Take great care here as visibility is poor, so listen as well as look. Follow Monk's Lane up past the Depot and curve right at the top into Neston. After 5½ miles (9km) turn left towards Atworth – a gentle descent with good views and wooded sections, but take care on the bend near the bottom.

7. At the junction with the A365 turn left, the right on to the Bradford Road. Bear left at the Forester's pub, go down the hill, straight through the crossroads, then bear left, signposted 'Holt 3'. Go straight past the 'Little Chalfield' sign then bear left down the dip, over the stream and up the other side. Turn left at the end, continue past Blackacre Farm and Leigh house, then follow the road round to the right.

At the end, turn left opposite the Tollgate pub and retrace your tracks to The Courts, taking extra care when turning right

PLACES OF INTEREST

The Courts
This is where local weavers once came to settle their disputes and, although the house is not open, the gardens are and feature a long herbaceous border, lily pond and small lake.
(See also page 50.)

Great Chalfield Manor
This moated Tudor manor (although the gatehouse is much earlier) features many fascinating artefacts. The Great Hall contains three masks set into the wall through which the women could secretly observe the goings-on in the room.
(See also page 15.)

Lacock
This National Trust site has a wealth of interesting buildings and exhibitions. Lacock Abbey

dates from 1232 and the house now on the site surrounds and incorporates much of the original buildings. Originally a medieval nunnery, the buildings survived the Dissolution of the Monasteries in 1539 and the Great Hall was rebuilt in Gothic style in the 18th century by the great-grandfather of Fox-Talbot, pioneer of photography.
(See page 54.)

Bradford-on-Avon
Originally a thriving textile centre, the town still has many interesting buildings, including a huge tithe barn, and the gaol, originally a chapel but later used to lock up the local drunks, situated on the old bridge. (See also page 14.) The town's oldest building, the tiny Saxon Church of St Lawrence, was originally built by St Aldhelm in about AD 700 as part of a monastery, which was later destroyed by the Danes.
(See also Cycle ride: The Canal and River at Bradford-on-Avon, pages 16–17.)

WHAT TO LOOK OUT FOR

The route runs through some unspoiled countryside offering a haven to many species of wildlife. If conditions are quiet you may well chance upon badgers or foxes, and some fields have large populations of rabbits. Most of the woodland is very old and well established, harbouring many types of native British birds, including finches, woodpeckers and thrushes.

LACOCK
WILTSHIRE. VILLAGE OFF A350,
3 MILES (5KM) S OF
CHIPPENHAM

One of the prettiest villages in the country, Lacock is mostly of stone, with some timber-framing. Lacock Abbey (see below) is an odd house, partly medieval, with 1550s alterations and a mock-medieval hall of 1754. Henry Fox Talbot, the pioneer photographer, lived here and the Fox Talbot Museum of Photography is based here. Lackham Gardens (see below) and the Museum of Vintage Farm Buildings are located to the north.

(See also Cycle ride: Holt and Lacock, pages 51–3.)

Lackham Country Attractions
3 MILES (5KM) S OF
CHIPPENHAM, ON A350
TEL: 01249 443111

Various visitor attractions are situated within the 520-acre (210-ha) estate of the Lackham College of Agriculture. Thatched and refurbished farm buildings accommodate the farm museum and the grounds feature a walled garden, glasshouses, rhododendron glades, riverside and woodland walks, a children's adventure playground and 5acres (2ha) of grassland devoted to rare breeds. There is a major collection of historical roses in the Italian Garden. Also grown here was the largest citron (large lemon) which earned a place in the *Guinness Book of Records*. The gardens have been extended to include a maze and gardens of the 17th, 18th and 19th centuries. For children, models of Rupert Bear and his friends can be seen in their new 'Nutwood.'

Open Etr–end Oct, certain days.

Lacock Abbey
TEL: 01249 730227

When Lacock was given to the National Trust in 1944 a whole village came as part of the gift, and a more delightful and complementary assemblage would be hard to find. The abbey was founded in 1232 and continued as an Augustinian nunnery until Henry VIII dissolved the monasteries in 1539. Like many other religious foundations, Lacock was converted into a private residence, but unlike most others it has retained a large proportion of its monastic buildings, including the cloisters, chapter house and sacristy. In general, Lacock was converted with care and sensitivity, though some of its features are Gothic Revival rather than pure medieval. It is furnished with some interesting pieces, including a chair which is said to have been used in the camp of Charles I, and a pair of 18th-century leather chests. Also on display is a photographic copy of the Lacock Abbey Magna Carta (the original is in the British Museum).

For most of its secular life Lacock Abbey was owned by the Talbot family, whose most famous member was William Henry Fox Talbot, the pioneer of photography who invented the photographic negative here. The middle window in the south gallery was the subject of Fox Talbot's earliest existing negative, and there is a Museum of Photography in the gatehouse.

Open Etr–Oct, every afternoon except Tuesday.

A single-street quarrying village, pronounced 'Lie', with one of the famous Somerset church towers. The whole church is basically 15th-century, with an elaborately decorated wooden roof.

(See also Feature: The Mendip Hills, pages 64–5.)

LEIGH UPON MENDIP
Somerset. Village off A361, 5 miles (8km) W of Frome

The largest known Roman temple in rural Britain was unearthed here in 1984. The manor itself was built in Norman times; its north front is on the site of a Saxon hall of the 11th century. The house has always been inhabited, and remains relatively untouched since the 19th century. Inside there are interpretative displays illustrating the history of the English manor house, the Civil War, and the ghosts and legends of Littledean Hall. The grounds offer beautiful walks, some of the oldest trees in Dean, fish pools in the walled garden and, of course, the Roman excavations. The house features an unusual history of ghosts and the supernatural. The most recent development at Littledean is a museum of hot-air balloons and airships.

Open: grounds and archaeological site, Apr–Oct, daily.

LITTLEDEAN HALL
Littledean, Gloucestershire
Tel: *01594 824213*

This large village just outside Bristol is noted for its huge park formed from the grounds of Ashton Court (the house is not open to the public). An important agricultural research establishment is situated near by.

LONG ASHTON
Somerset. Village off B3128, 3 miles (5km) SW of Bristol

The man who built Longleat was truly remarkable. In the space of just 40 years John Thynne rose from working in Henry VIII's kitchen to entertaining Queen Elizabeth I at his vast mansion. Ambitious and persuasive, he acquired both social position and great wealth and laid the foundations of a dynasty which still occupies the vast country

LONGLEAT
Wiltshire. 5 miles (8km) W of Warminster. Entrance on Warminster–Frome road, A362
Tel: *01985 844400*

Tigers at Longleat Safari Park

estate originally purchased for £53. When the new house, which he designed himself, was destroyed by fire the determined Thynne simply bought a quarry of Bath stone and started again.

Colourful characters have always populated Longleat. John Thynne's son, a lazy and violent man, was fined for fraud and the mismanagement of his public duties; a later heir married a woman who, though of noble birth, was so disreputable that her behaviour shocked even Charles II and she was banned from court; the next heir was murdered by assassins hired by an admirer of his wife; another eloped with the daughter of a local toll-keeper. The first Viscount Weymouth, however, was a more worthy descendant of Thynne. Of modest habits and a devoted husband, he built up the estate and created wonderful gardens, sadly destroyed in one generation by his successor who neglected both house and grounds. The third Viscount found favour at the Court of George III, who elevated him to the rank of Marquess of Bath and visited Longleat in 1789. Nevertheless he died in debt and his son, a shrewd businessman, was forced to concentrate all his effort on saving the estate. He also made substantial improvement to the house, employing James Wyatt to carry out the work which took ten years to complete.

In the history of such a family as this it is difficult to pick out a 'Golden Age', but the Victorian era certainly left its mark here. The estate prospered, high society was lavishly entertained and the state rooms were remodelled in baroque style, with no expense spared. The excellent workmanship is still evident today in the

superbly intricate gilded ceilings and the extraordinarily sumptuous and richly decorated rooms, and the fully restored Victorian kitchens offer an interesting glimpse of life 'below stairs'. But the development of Longleat did not stop there – the present Lord Bath's apartments are decorated with his own murals, hugely colourful works which display a characteristic lack of restraint.

The magnificent grounds, laid out by 'Capability' Brown, offer many lovely walks. The estate has become equally famous for the safari park, which is home to hundreds of wild animals including Britain's only white tiger. There is also a maze and narrow-gauge railway, and boat trips are available.

Open all year; house daily, safari park Mar–Nov. Closed Xmas.

LYDIARD PARK

LYDIARD TREGOZE, WILTSHIRE. NEAR M4 EXIT 6. FOLLOW BROWN TOURIST INFORMATION SIGNS.
TEL: 01793 770401

Set in beautiful country parkland, this fine Georgian house belonged to the St John family for 500 years until 1943 when the house and parkland were purchased by the Swindon Corporation. Since then the sadly dilapidated house has been gradually restored and refurbished with period furniture (in many cases original to the house) and a large St John family portrait collection (also original). Exceptional plasterwork, early wallpaper, a rare painted glass window, and a room devoted to the talented 18th-century amateur artist, Lady Diana Spencer, can also be seen. Adjacent, the church of St Mary's has many fine and unusual memorials to the St John family. The Park, now operating as a Country Park, offers a variety of pleasant woodland walks, spacious lawns, lakes and a children's adventure playground.

House open all year, certain times. Closed Good Fri & Xmas.

Park open all year, daily.

MALMESBURY

WILTSHIRE. TOWN ON B4640, 10 MILES (16KM) N OF CHIPPENHAM

This ancient settlement grew up around the abbey, which was founded in the 7th century and became famous under St Aldhelm, who died in 709. His shrine attracted many pilgrims and the church was rebuilt on a huge scale in the 12th century. The huge ruins and church which survive display some of the finest Norman architecture and sculpture in the country, but they are not the complete building: a huge spire fell down in about 1500, and a tower also collapsed.

The town has one of the finest market crosses in the country, elaborate and dating from about 1500. Its 17th-century cottages and some almshouses recall the time when Malmesbury was a weaving centre, and there are handsome Georgian houses and cottages and a big 18th-century silk mill on the river. The Athelstan Museum in the town hall relates the local history.

Charlton Park House, 2 miles (3km) north-east, is of 1607 and the 1770s and has only a few rooms open.

Opposite
The magnificent façade of Longleat House

Grid ref: ST933875

INFORMATION

The walk is 2 miles (3km) long,
level, easy walking, apart from
the steps leaving the town.
A few stiles.
Refreshment facilities in
Malmesbury.
Picnic site by weir, near station
car park.
Toilets in Malmesbury.

START

Malmesbury is 10 miles (16km)
north of Chippenham on the
B4640. Start the walk from the
Station Road car park.

*This undemanding walk starts from the
historic town of Malmesbury which,
with its narrow, hilly streets, ancient stone
buildings and numerous craft and
antique shops, is a fascinating place to
explore on foot.*

DIRECTIONS

From the car park follow the
signpost to the town centre. Cross
the River Avon and go up the
steps at the back of the abbey
then turn right into the abbey
garden. Walk across to the far

right corner by the Old Bell Hotel.
Cross the road and turn left. Go
underneath the large mirror and
follow the lane. Turn right at the
bottom of the steps and continue

Malmesbury Abbey

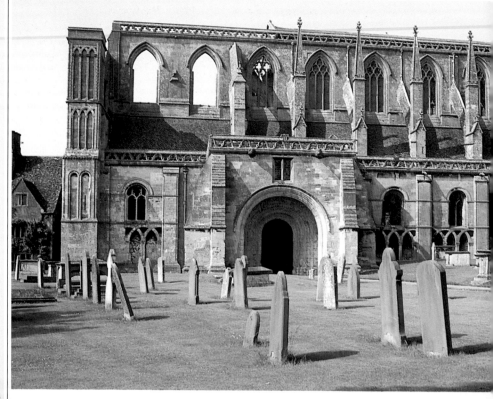

down the lane ('Burnivale') until the path opens into a wider lane. Here turn left down the lane towards the river and go over two bridges, passing the weir on the left. After crossing a metal stile turn almost immediately to the left, away from the river bank. Cross a small flat stone bridge and follow a clear path to the right to reach a farm lane. Turn left, pass a barn on the right, and continue ahead. Pass to the right of an old stone building and through the gate. Cut diagonally across the field to the tree in the top right-hand corner opposite. Cross the improvised stile to the right of this

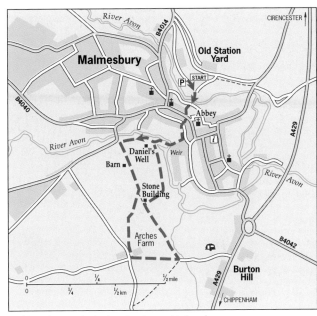

and head towards the big Dutch barn. Follow the diagonal path across to the farmyard. Go straight through the yard and turn sharp left down the farm road. At the bottom of this road go through the gate on the left and follow the path round the bottom of the field. Just before the old buildings passed earlier, turn right across a stile and turn left at the bottom of the field. Go through the gap at the bottom of the wall, over the stone slab bridge, and retrace your steps back up to the abbey and the car park.

Malmesbury

Built on a hill by the River Avon in Saxon times, Malmesbury (see page 57) was officially recognised in the *Guinness Book of Records* as the oldest borough in England. At the top of the town is the famous 12th-century abbey; only the nave remains today. Malmesbury is another Wiltshire town that has retained its blind house (see Bradford-on-Avon, page 14). There are two here – one on either side of the arched gateway leading from the market place into the abbey ground.

WHAT TO LOOK OUT FOR

Evidence of prisoners' desperate and futile attempts to escape can be seen in the scratched stone by the keyholes of one of the 'blind houses'.

59

MARLBOROUGH

WILTSHIRE. TOWN ON A4, 10 MILES (16KM) S OF SWINDON

Marlborough is famous for its handsome wide High Street, lined with attractive buildings and colonnades – one of the finest market town streets in the country, with Marlborough College (a public school founded in 1843) and a medieval church at one end, and the classical town hall of 1900 and another church at the other. The Merchant's House of 1656 is being made into a museum. To the north are the rolling Marlborough Downs, with many racehorses.

MEARE

SOMERSET. VILLAGE ON B3151, 4 MILES (6KM) NW OF GLASTONBURY

Once an island on the Somerset Levels, Meare has a little medieval Fish House, used to process fish caught in the surrounding lakes. Extraordinarily elaborate late medieval iron hinges can be seen on the church door.

MELKSHAM

WILTSHIRE. TOWN OFF A350, 6 MILES (10KM) S OF CHIPPENHAM

Melksham is a small town on the River Avon, with a surprising amount of industry and a sizeable 15th-century church. Mostly modern in the centre, it has older buildings around the church and some Regency houses from a small spa which first opened in 1815.

Above: Marlborough College

*T*he route begins at Marlborough and takes in a number of small picturesque villages and wooded valleys. It also follows part of the peaceful Kennet and Avon Canal, passing several interesting places to visit. The cycling is relatively easy for the most part, but there are two short, steep climbs and two fast, steep descents where particular care will be needed; beware of mud or loose gravel on the lanes.

INFORMATION

Total distance
26 miles (41.5km)

Difficulty
Moderate

OS Map
Landranger 1:50,000 sheets 173 (Swindon and Devizes) and 174 (Newbury and Wantage)

Tourist Information
Marlborough, tel: 01672 513989

Nearest railway station
Bedwyn; also Pewsey and Hungerford

Refreshments
Marlborough offers a wide variety of pubs and cafés, including the excellent Polly Tea Rooms on the High Street. Along the route, pubs include The Red Lion at Axford (good food), and The Cross Keys in Great Bedwyn, which welcomes children and has

special secure facilities for cycles. There are good picnic spots to be found beside the canal, or in Savernake Forest.

(See also Great Bedwyn, page 44, and Savernake Forest, page 76.)

START

The route starts in the small town of Marlborough, where the A4 and A436 meet, south of Swindon. Parking is usually available in the wide main street; alternatively, park in one of the public parks.

Marlborough's broad main street

DIRECTIONS

1. From the centre of Marlborough head east along the main street towards Hungerford. At the end bear left to pass the Imperial Cancer Research Fund shop, and take the first turn right into Silverless Street. Follow this to the end, and go straight across into St Martins, signed to Mildenhall, Aldbourne and Ramsbury. Follow this minor road through the outskirts of Marlborough, and enjoy a short

61

descent to the river, crossing the bridge at the bottom. The road then rises gently, with good views of the River Kennet to your right. Cross over the disused railway bridge, and follow the road for 1 mile (1.5km) to Mildenhall. Pass the Horseshoes on the left. Follow the road round to the right and continue on this road beside the river towards Ramsbury. Continue past Durnsford Mill and the Granary Kitchen tea rooms, to reach Axford.

2. Pedal up the rise and through Axford, past the church, and enjoy the views of the river and meadows below. Stay on this road as it veers away from the river and at the fork, bear right, following signs for Ramsbury. Follow the undulating road through the wood, looking out for Ramsbury Manor on the right. After a long straight descent, the road bends left into Ramsbury.

3. Follow the High Street to pass a row of houses with a brick-and-lint façade. At the end of the High Street fork right, then take the next right turn, signed 'Froxfield'. Cross the bridge (look out for ducks) to embark on a short but steep climb through the Z-bends. At the next junction turn left, still signed to Froxfield. After 2 undulating miles (3km) the road narrows, leading into Froxfield. Take care on the narrow bends as you reach the village. Continue to meet the main road (A4).

4. Bear left here, towards Hungerford; pass a long row of almshouses, to turn right after The Pelican pub, signposted to Little Bedwyn. Cross the railway bridge, then the bridge over the canal, then bear right to follow the Kennet and Avon canal for about 1½ miles (2.5km) to Little Bedwyn. Follow the brick wall round to the left, and then turn

right for Great Bedwyn. Cross over the railway bridge then bear left for Great Bedwyn. Turn left at The Three Tuns as you come into the village, then turn right into Church Street, opposite the Cross Keys.

5. Continue on Church Street, passing the unusual Stone Museum (see also page 44). Shortly after leaving the village turn right, signposted 'Crofton' (rather than go over the railway bridge), and continue parallel with the railway. Head into Crofton, past the thatched cottages and up the rise, to pass the Crofton Beam Engines (see also page 34). Follow the road over the railway bridge – you are now between the railway and the canal. The road swings over the canal bridge, then bear right towards Wolfhall and Burbage.

The canal near Great Bedwyn

Climb up through the farmyard complex at Wolfhall and go on to Burbage. Bear right through the outskirts of the village and turn right on to the main street.

6. After ½ mile (1km) turn right at The Three Horseshoes at Stibb Green, and follow this road for ¼ mile (0.5km) past the Savernake Forest Hotel, and over the railway line. Start the gentle climb out of the valley, looking across the deer park, right, to see Tottenham House. A short way further on, turn left opposite a brick and ironwork gateway, into Savernake Forest. (See also page 76.) Follow this road for 3 miles (5km) straight through the forest, passing through the gates at the far end. Turn left on to the A4 towards Marlborough, passing the Savernake Hospital, and drop down the long, steep descent into Marlborough. Bear right at the first roundabout, and left at the second, back into the town centre.

PLACES OF INTEREST

Marlborough
From the lively mix of buildings along Marlborough's broad High Street, you could be forgiven for believing this a Georgian market town. A foray down almost any side street however reveals the wooden timbering of much earlier houses. In fact, much more of the town would have been timbered and thatched, like the surrounding

WHAT TO LOOK OUT FOR

Some of the churches along the route contain unexpected delights. The church at Mildenhall, unusually, was completely refitted inside early in the 19th century, and remains a microcosm of that age in oak, including box-pews. A church has stood on the same spot in Ramsbury since Anglo-Saxon times, and fragments of wonderfully carved stone memorials dating from that period may still be seen there today. Look out too, for the chandeliers in the church – rather more modern, as they are 18th-century additions.

villages, but a series of major fires in the 17th century resulted in a thatching ban. It is a pleasing place, dominated at its western end by the famous public school, Marlborough College, and with lots of interesting old corners to explore. (See also page 60.)

Froxfield
The almshouses of this little village were the gift in 1694 of Sarah, the dowager Duchess of Somerset, to house poor widows. The story of 'Wild' Darrell is also linked with Froxfield – accused of throwing a new-born baby on to a fire, he was pursued by the Hounds of Hell.

The Kennet and Avon Canal
This scenic waterway was once a main thoroughfare for transporting goods across southern England. Nowadays the boats travel strictly for pleasure, and it is hard to imagine a more relaxing way to see the countryside than from the top of a narrow-boat gliding

steadily along. In times past the canal would have been a lifeline to the villages along its length such as Little and Great Bedwyn. Beyond Great Bedwyn, look out for the Crofton Beam Engine, a steam-driven engine which was built to pump water to the summit level of the canal. (See also pages 34 and 44.)

Savernake Forest
Great oaks, elms and beeches dominate this beautiful ancient forest, dating back over 900 years. Once a royal forest, Jane Seymour was the daughter of one of its wardens, and celebrated her wedding to Henry VIII at nearby Wolfhall. Rare wild flowers grow under the shady canopy of the woods, and forest glades provide ideal picnic spots. The Column, visible through the trees near the south-east end of the Grand Avenue, was raised to mark George III's recovery from madness. (See also page 76.)

THE MENDIP HILLS

The steep sides of the Ebbor Gorge National Nature Reserve are covered by woodland, predominantly ash and oak

The Mendip Hills, honeycombed by caves and exploited for centuries by lead mining, rise in a great limestone barrier above the Somerset Levels and the Bristol Channel.

From Weston-Super-Mare and the Bristol Channel, the imposing 984-ft (300-m) high ridge of the Mendips sweeps eastwards to the Chew Valley and Wells. It is the southernmost outcrop of Carboniferous limestone in the country, and famous for its show caves such as those in the Cheddar Gorge and at Wookey Hole (see pages 28 and 93). Designated in 1972, the Mendip Hills Area of Outstanding Natural Beauty (AONB) covers 76.5 square miles (198 sq km) of Somerset. The sheer rock faces of the gorge sides are home to rare flora such as the beautiful Cheddar pink (see page 28).

The Mendips contain two National Nature Reserves, the beautiful limestone woodlands of the Ebbor Gorge and the famous ash woods of Rodney Stoke, and many Sites of Special Scientific Interest. These lime-rich habitats are very rare nationally and particularly so in the south-west. The limestone gorges of the Mendips, such as Cheddar and Ebbor on the southern flanks and Burrington Combe on the northern slopes, were cut by the tremendous force of melt water from retreating Ice-Age glaciers. Features unique to limestone country are the sink-holes and depressions where water has sunk below the surface, the dew-ponds and the spectacular caves.

The whole area is very rich in archaeological remains, with barrows, field systems, settlements and earthworks dating from the Bronze Age. The earliest settlers used the caves in the limestone for their homes and for shelter, as discoveries at Gough's Cave in the Cheddar Gorge have proved. Among the most impressive prehistoric sites is Dolebury Camp, a two-tiered Iron-Age hill-fort overlooking the village of Churchill and the Bristol Channel at the western end of the range.

At the highest point of Dolebury Camp are the remains of a warrener's house, and the long, barrow-like earthworks found on top of the Mendips often turn out to be the pillow mounds constructed in medieval times to encourage the newly introduced meat-producing rabbits to breed. Since Roman times, as in many other limestone areas, the Mendips were important as a centre for lead mining, and the evidence is still to be seen on the open hills in the patches of disturbed ground and old mines and adits (shafts that are almost horizontal) known locally as 'gruffy ground'.

The mainstay of farming on the tops of the Mendips is sheep farming, and Priddy Fair is still the major show for the shepherds to show off the best of their breeding flocks. Lower down the slopes, dairy and mixed farming becomes more important, with horticultural holdings on the more fertile southern fringe.

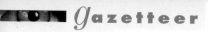

MIDSOMER NORTON
SOMERSET. TOWN ON A362,
1 MILE (2KM) W OF RADSTOCK

This town is not as pretty as its name, being situated in the middle of the old coal-mining area, with tips and remains of collieries all around. The unusual 17th-century church tower has a statue of Charles II, and a converted medieval barn houses a Roman Catholic church.

MONKTON COMBE
SOMERSET. VILLAGE OFF A36,
2 MILES (3KM) SE OF BATH

To the east of this stone village is the famous Dundas Aqueduct, opened in 1805 to carry the Kennet and Avon Canal over the River Avon 60 feet (18m) below.

NAILSEA
SOMERSET. SMALL TOWN ON
B3130, 7 MILES (11KM)
W OF BRISTOL

The coal mined here was used in the 19th century for the large glass industry, which has since disappeared. Now the town consists mostly of suburban housing.

NORTHLEACH COTSWOLD
COUNTRYSIDE COLLECTION
FOSSEWAY, 12 MILES (19KM)
E OF CHELTENHAM ON A429
TEL: 01451 860715

The story of everyday rural life in the Cotswolds is told in this museum, housed in the remaining buildings of the Northleach House of Correction. It was one of a group of Gloucestershire's 'country prisons' built around 1789 by Sir Onesiphorus Paul. The Lloyd-Baker agricultural collection, one of the best in the country, exhibits a unique collection of Gloucestershire harvest-wagons. There is a 'below stairs' gallery showing a dairy, kitchen and laundry. There are also special exhibitions. Workshops on rag-rug making, felt making, patchwork, natural dyeing and basket making are held.

Open Apr–Nov, daily, certain times. Some winter opening.

NUNNEY
SOMERSET. VILLAGE OFF A361,
3 MILES (5KM) SW OF FROME

It is not often a village can add a moated medieval castle to a list of ingredients that already satisfies every requirement of a fairy-tale village. But Nunney is exceptional. It is set in a wooded valley at the eastern end of the Mendip Hills; a stream flows past the grey-stone, red-tiled houses and thatched cottages; there is a church on the hill, a fine manor house and a pub. It even has a thatched bus shelter.

The castle dates to 1373, when Sir John Delamare, recently returned from the war in France with much booty, was given a licence to fortify and crenellate his manse. He placed four mighty, round towers at the corners of a rectangular central block four storeys high. Pevsner says it is of a type found in the north of England; others say it was modelled on the Bastille in France. (See Nunney Castle, page 71.) Today the romantic ruin, in the care of English Heritage, is reached from the main street by a footbridge over what is said to be the deepest water-filled moat in the country. Across the stream and the street from the castle is the church, originally 13th-century but much rebuilt in the 19th century. It has a round Norman font, parts of a Saxon cross and a wall-painting of St George. There are effigies of Sir

John (probably) and of subsequent owners of the castle, the Poulets and the Praters. One of the Roundhead cannonballs that wrecked the castle is on display. The Nunney Brook flows down the length of the village and it was this that first brought the village prosperity, when the wool trade was centred on nearby Frome in the late 17th and early 18th centuries. Many of the weavers' cottages in Horn Street carry dates within this period and most of the bigger houses were also built at this time, including Palladian-style Manor Farm. Wool was washed on the sloping cobbled pavement in front of the church, where the medieval market cross stands. The industry declined locally towards the end of the 18th century when mills in the North took all the trade, but at about that time Fussell's ironworks grew up, using the Nunney Brook for power and providing employment well into the 19th century.

'The Village of Nunney ... perfection, having everything which the heart could desire to make it both lovely and interesting ...'
MAXWELL FRASER

Looking towards Nunney's main street from the castle footbridge

W inding between pretty Somerset villages, this route leads through the bustling market town of Frome and back out into rolling countryside, returning via a picturesque moated castle.

INFORMATION

Total distance
15½ miles (25km)

Difficulty
Moderate

OS Map
Landranger 1:50,000 sheet 183
(Yeovil & Frome)

Tourist Information
Frome, tel: 01373 467271

Cycle shops/hire
D J Cycles, Frome, tel: 01373 453563

Nearest railway station
Frome

Refreshments
Pubs along the route include The George at Nunney, The Fox and Hounds at Tytherington and The Talbot Inn at Mells; cafés and tea rooms, as well as Scoffs, in Frome.

Nunney Castle, with the village across the moat

START

The route starts in the village of Nunney, 3 miles (5km) south-west of Frome, just north of the A361. Park in the village centre car park.

DIRECTIONS

1. From the village centre car park head uphill away from the river, following signs to Witham Friary and Bruton. At the top of the rise turn down the side of The Theobald Arms, following the cycleway signs. Pass under the major road (A361), and bear left towards Trudoxhill. Go into Trudoxhill, passing The White Hart pub and bear right for

Witham and Gare Hill. Just up the following rise, take the right fork for Witham and at the T-junction turn left. Stay on this road, downhill, for about a mile, crossing the River Frome, and eventually running parallel with the railway line. Turn left at the junction signposted to Nunney, and after ¼ mile (0.5km) bear right into a small lane. At the crossroads turn right, pass through the hamlet of Lower Marston, and turn left at the end for Tytherington.

2. Pass the site on the left of the former village of Marston, to reach Tytherington. Continue through the village, past The Fox and Hounds, to take the next fork right. Go through a kissing gate, and cycle up the route of the old road. At the far end go through another kissing gate, and cross over the A361 with great care. On the opposite side, take the left fork and climb up the lane. At the end of the lane go straight across into the 'No Through Road', and continue down the side of The Mason's Arms. Continue down this road, squeezing through the bollards at the end, and carry on through the residential area, going straight over each junction to reach Nunney Road. (To take a short-cut straight back to Nunney, turn left here and follow the road down to the car park in the centre of Nunney). Turn right, and at the T-junction go right again, on to the main A362. At the

roundabout turn left, and head down into Frome town centre.

3. Cross the river bridge and climb up the hill the other side, taking the second turning left into Welshmill Road. Follow this road into Lower Innox, and climb up through a housing estate. Pass The Farmer's Arms pub, go over the humpbacked bridge, and at the junction turn left. Follow the road under the railway, and climb gently to the A362. Turn right on to the main road, and almost immediately left, signposted to Hapsford and Great Elm. Follow this road through Great Elm and down into Mells. At the junction at the bottom, bear right and climb up through the village past the war memorial.

4. Pass the Talbot Inn and take the next turning left, past the Rectory and down a steep hill. Turn right at the bottom and follow the river for a short distance. Where the road continues round to the right, turn left, climbing up from the entrance to Mells Park and past the village school. At the top go straight over the junction, heading for Chantry, and in the village, go straight over the crossroads. The road descends steeply, with a following steep but short climb. Bear left at the top, and continue over the next junction, towards Nunney. At the T-junction bear right, and drop down back into the village centre to return to the car park.

PLACES OF INTEREST

Nunney Castle

This spectacular ruin is to the north of the village. Originally a narrow rectangle in shape, with great corner towers, some say it was modelled on the Bastille in France. The castle dates back to 1373 and was built by Sir John Delamare, whose tomb is in the village church; he adapted his existing deep-moated manor house, adding crenellations and fortifications. In 1645 the then owner, sir Richard Prater (whose family are also represented in the church), was besieged in the castle with his followers. The Parliamentarian army succeeded

WHAT TO LOOK OUT FOR

Along the route there are various signs of much earlier settlements, long deserted. At the junction near Tytherington stood the village of Marston – now the sister villages of Marston Bigot, Marston Gate and Lower Marston are all that survive. On the road to Mells, the earth ramparts of the prehistoric camp at Tedbury are still as high as 15ft (4.5m) in some places; Wadbury Camp, also to the left of this road, is also passed.

in damaging the castle beyond repair, and it has lain deserted ever since. Houses in the pretty village mostly date to the 1600s or 1700s. (See also page 71.)

Frome

This busy market town on the River Frome (pronounced 'Froom') is well worth exploring on foot. Of its narrow side-streets the most appealing – and most famous – is Cheap Street, with its steep roofs, timbered buildings and narrow runnel of water down the centre of the road. The almshouses near the bridge date from the early 18th century; the parish church was heavily and controversially restored in Victorian times. (See page 39.)

Mells

Frequently described as one of Somerset's loveliest villages, Mells combines pretty thatched cottages and pleasing stone houses with a spattering of small greens and a practical, lived-in air. Mells Manor, a Tudor mansion, was the abode of the Homer family. According to legend, the deeds to the manor were hidden in a pie and sent to Henry VIII, but were stolen along the way; this tale is celebrated in the nursery rhyme 'Little Jack Horner'!

Mells seen from the church tower

In 1645 Cromwell's men set up a cannon on high ground near Nunney, preparing to lay siege to a castle which was at the time held for Charles I. Almost immediately, a hole was made in the north wall, just above the entrance, and Cromwell's troops continued firing to widen the breach. Two days later the castle garrison surrendered and the Parliamentarian soldiers swarmed into Nunney, looting and removing everything of value. The damaged wall remained standing until 1910, when it collapsed into the moat, blocking it up. The moat was later cleared, and it is fed today by the small stream that runs through this pretty Somerset village.

Nunney was built by Sir John Delamare in 1373. By this time, the church had already been built in the best position in the village, and so the castle is sited on a stretch of land that most castle-builders would have rejected as too low. But Delamare was perhaps not so much interested in building a strongly defensible fortress as a splendid palace that would reflect his own rising glory (he late became Sheriff of Somerset and a Knight of the Shire). It is a roughly oblong building, more reminiscent of a French château than an English castle, and is an attractive feature of a delightful village.

Open at any reasonable time.

NUNNEY CASTLE
3½ MILES (5.5KM) SW OF FROME, OFF A361

The towers of Nunney Castle, still daunting even in ruins

Grid ref: ST609925

INFORMATION

The walk is 3 miles (5km) long. No road walking and no gradients, but very muddy in places. Several stiles and one gate to climb. Pubs in Oldbury.

START

Oldbury lies on the south bank of the River Severn about 3 miles (5km) north of the Severn Bridge. Parking is available in the Church Road car park, which is located by the bridge, opposite the Anchor Inn.

A n undemanding walk on absolutely level ground, with the Severn estuary providing interest for the first part – it is well worth taking binoculars.

DIRECTIONS

After leaving the car park, go through the pedestrian gate to the right, signposted 'Thornbury Sailing Club'. Follow the road to the clubhouse, passing the sluice gates to the left, and turn right along the sea wall. Continue for about ¾ mile (1km), with the nuclear power station looming ahead. When you reach the power station, turn right along the signposted path until you reach a road.

Turn right here, then shortly right again, where the path is signposted, and climb the gate into a field (there are usually cattle here). Follow the left-hand field edge to a stile by a ruined

A creek near the Severn Bridge

72

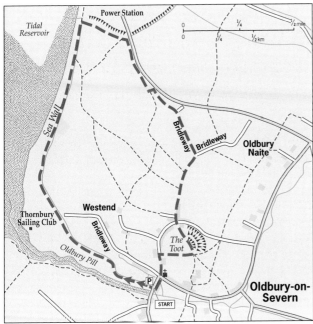

The Toot

Oldbury Camp, otherwise known as The Toot, is an Iron-Age hill-fort. Covering about 10 acres (4.5ha), it has a double bank and ditch on the north and east sides, and a single bank on the west. The discovery of coins here indicates that it was in use in Roman times, too. Now it is an integral part of the village; footpaths cross it and it is partially encircled by streets and housing.

Oldbury Church

Perched on a hill in the flat plain alongside the Severn, Oldbury's church can be seen for miles around and provides a useful landmark throughout the walk. It is dedicated to Arilda, who was a local saint in Saxon times. The only other church in the country bearing her name is at Oldbury-on-the-Hill, about 15 miles (24km) away. Views from the churchyard are superb, and it is possibly to make out the route of the walk from here.

building and continue on to two gates. Go through the left-hand gate, then turn right along the track just before reaching the road. This bridleway can be very muddy indeed.

At the point where the track divides, turn right. The lane turns into a metalled road. Continue to the fork and take the public footpath signposted almost ahead, between houses. Cross two stiles before reaching The Toot. Cross the double stile in the right-hand corner and continue straight ahead to a stile hidden in the hedge. Cross this and head for the stone stile between stone walls.

Continue to steps and the road. Turn left past The Ship, then cross into Church Road.

WHAT TO LOOK OUT FOR

There is always something to watch on the river estuary, with all manner of craft including tugboats, dredgers and sailing dinghies from the Thornbury Sailing Club. Birdwatchers will find plenty to interest them, and with luck will see cormorants at any time of the year. The Severn is an important refuge for winter visitors which may include dunlin, curlew, and ringed plover.

Ringed Plover

The nuclear power station at Oldbury-on-Severn

OLDBURY-ON-SEVERN
GLOUCESTERSHIRE. VILLAGE OFF
B4061, 2 MILES (3KM) NW
OF THORNBURY

A scattered village with fine views over the Severn Bridge and nuclear power station. The church is worth visiting for the art nouveau glass in the east window.
(See also Walk: Oldbury-on-Severn, pages 72–3.)

OWLPEN MANOR
GLOUCESTERSHIRE. 3 MILES
(5KM) E OF DURSLEY OFF
B4066, FOLLOW BROWN
TOURIST INFORMATION SIGNS
TEL: 01453 860261

This romantic Tudor manor house, dating from 1450 to 1616, contains unique 17th-century painted cloth wallhangings, furniture, pictures and textiles. There is an Arts and Crafts collection. The house is set in formal terraced gardens, and is part of a picturesque Cotswold manorial group including a Jacobean Court House, a watermill dating from 1728 (now holiday cottages), a Victorian church and medieval tithe barn.
Open Apr–Oct, certain days, afternoons only.

PORTISHEAD
SOMERSET. TOWN ON A369,
8 MILES (13KM) W OF BRISTOL

A little medieval village on the Bristol Channel, which became a tiny seaside resort from early Victorian times and then developed with Avonmouth (see page 6), to replace Bristol's docks. The huge Royal Portbury Dock at the mouth of the River Avon opened in 1977, with the largest dock-gates in Britain at that time.

RADSTOCK
SOMERSET. TOWN ON A367,
8 MILES (13KM) SW OF BATH

A hilly little coal-mining town, very industrial for the Avon countryside. The Radstock, Midsomer Norton and District Museum is housed in a converted 18th-century barn (see page 75).

This local history museum, run by volunteers, is housed in the 18th-century barn of a former dairy and cheese-making farm located in the old North Somerset coalfield. Features include a reconstructed coalface, miner's cottage, model railway, agricultural implements, a 1930s Co-op shop, a blacksmith's shop, mining photographs, chapel china and leisure bygones. There is also a Victorian schoolroom. Temporary exhibitions are held throughout the year.

Open Jan–Nov, Sat, Sun & BHs certain times.

A stone village with two churches, one the original medieval, the other a strange, turreted building of 1824, supposedly built for the Wiltshire part of the parish, then split between the two counties.

Rode Bird Gardens consist of 17 acres (7ha) of grounds, planted with trees, shrubs, and flower gardens, in a pretty and little-visited village. The bird collection consists of around 1,200 birds of 200 different species, and there is also a clematis collection, an ornamental lake, a Pets' Corner, a children's play area and an information centre. Plants are for sale. Children must be accompanied by an adult. A woodland steam railway operates daily from Easter until the beginning of October, weather permitting.

Open all year, daily. Closed Xmas.

Radstock, Midsomer Norton & District Museum
Barton Meade House, Haydon. 1 mile (1.5km) S on Haydon–Kilmersden road
Tel: 01761 437722

RODE
Somerset. Village off A361, 4 miles (6km) NE of Frome.

Rode Bird Gardens
Off A36 between Bath and Warminster
Tel: 01373 830326

A peacock in the extensive Bird Gardens at Rode

SALISBURY PLAIN
WILTSHIRE. SCENIC AREA N OF SALISBURY

The Plain is 20 miles (30km) by 12 miles (20km), grassy downland from prehistoric times until World War I, when it was ploughed up. Now a huge area of empty chalkland, virtually without villages and ringed by towns, it is much used by the army for training. There are many prehistoric remains, most famously those of Stonehenge (see page 79).

SAVERNAKE FOREST
WILTSHIRE. SCENIC AREA ON A4, SE OF MARLBOROUGH

An enormous area of woodland, formerly a medieval hunting forest, with the Grand Avenue flanked by huge old beech trees. Straight rides cut right across it, one with a column of 1781; this is wonderful walking country. Tottenham House (limited opening) is a huge mansion of 1825, with a lavish church of 1861, at St Katherine's.

SHEPTON MALLET
SOMERSET. TOWN OFF A37, 18 MILES (29KM) S OF BRISTOL

Savernake Forest provides excellent walking country

In the centre of this small, mostly stone-built town there is an elaborate market cross, and wooden medieval market stalls. The church has a fine Somerset tower, and perhaps the finest wagon roof in the country, with angels, 350 panels and bosses. Brewing has been an important industry, with a big Victorian brewery on the outskirts. Babycham is made here. The museum contains exhibits of local interest.

Gazetteer

▶ One of the most impressive archaeological monuments in the country – a mound 550 feet (167m) across the base and 130 feet (39m) high, with a ditch round it. It is part of the Avebury complex of sites (see page 5), and probably dates from the neolithic period.

▶ Founded in 1946 by the late Sir Peter Scott, Slimbridge is now the home of the world's largest collection of exotic wildfowl and the only place in Europe where all six types of flamingo can be seen. Up to 8,000 wild birds winter on the 800-acre (324ha) reserve of flat fields, marsh and mudflats on the River Severn. First-class viewing facilities are available, and in winter the towers and hides provide remarkable views of the migratory birds. Other features include a permanent indoor interactive exhibit, with videos, a computer game and large tanks with coral reef fish, freshwater fish, and peatland plants, and a Tropical House. There is a packed programme of events and activities throughout the year, including evening talks and guided walks. Facilities for the disabled include free wheelchair loan, purpose-built toilets for wheelchair users and a taped audio guide.

Open all year, daily. Closed Xmas.

SILBURY HILL
WILTSHIRE. VILLAGE ON A4, 1 MILE (2KM) S OF AVEBURY

SLIMBRIDGE
WWT SLIMBRIDGE GLOUCESTERSHIRE OFF A38, SIGNED FROM M5 JUNCTIONS 13 & 14 TEL: 01453 890333 & 890065

Slimbridge is world famous for its collection of flamingos

SOUTH CADBURY
SOMERSET. VILLAGE OFF A303, 2 MILES (3KM) E OF SPARKFORD

▶ This stone village in lovely countryside is best known for Cadbury Castle, a big Iron-Age hill-fort, woody and with good views. It has been traditionally associated with King Arthur, and excavations in the 1960s showed that the hill-fort had been re-occupied in the 5th and 6th centuries, the time of the 'real' King Arthur.

STANWAY
GLOUCESTERSHIRE VILLAGE OFF B4077, 4 MILES (6KM) NE OF WINCHCOMBE

▶ This picturesque place of stone and thatched cottages stands at the foot of wooded Stanway Hill. Playwright James Barrie designed its cricket pavilion, and Eric Gill carved lettering on its war memorial. Near the church stands a huge medieval tithe barn and the impressive 17th-century gatehouse of Stanway House (see below), a repository of fine furniture and paintings.

Stanway House
TEL: 01386 584469

▶ Built of golden limestone when Queen Elizabeth I was on the throne, Stanway House is not only an outstanding example of Jacobean architecture, it is also a fascinating portrayal of the development of the manor house of a Cotswold squire. Richard Tracy, whose family had owned land in the county since before the Conquest, obtained the lease from the Abbot of Tewkesbury in 1530 – the only time that Stanway has changed hands in the last 1,260 years. It is now the home of Lord and Lady Neidpath whose ancestor, Lord Elcho, married

The fine, pillared 17th-century gateway at Stanway House

the last Tracy heiress. It is said that he died of an overdose of punch.

There is a sense of continuity at Stanway; it is still very much a lived-in family home and remains the heart of the community. Having resisted the temptation to sell off its cottages, it is one of very few estates to which tenants bring their rent in person on a quarterly basis, handing over the sums due at a 250-year-old table in the Audit Room. The tour of this beautiful house is taken under the watchful eye of generations of family portraits, people who have helped to preserve and perpetuate what is one of the most romantic houses in Britain.

Open Jun–Sep, selected afternoons.

Stonehenge is one of the most famous prehistoric monuments in Europe and has been the source of endless speculation by archaeologists and others. The henge was started about 5,000 years ago, but was redesigned several times during the following 1,500 years. The earliest parts are an encircling ditch and bank which were made about 2800 BC. About 700 years later, huge Blue Stones, 80 in all and each weighing 2 tons, were brought from south-west Wales. However, before the work on these was finished, enormous sarsen stones weighing over 50 tons each were dragged from the Marlborough Downs and the whole structure was reorganised into the

New stables were built at Stanway in 1859. The original block, to the east of the barn and next to the churchyard, was abandoned because worshippers were disturbed by 'the oaths of the strappers'.

STONEHENGE
2 MILES (3KM) W OF AMESBURY, AT THE JUNCTION OF A303 AND A344/A360 TEL: 01980 624715

There can be few sites in England more evocative than Stonehenge

design we see today. This is made up of an outer ring with mortis-and-tenon-fitted lintels and an inner horseshoe of five pairs of uprights with lintels. Later on, the Blue Stones were re-erected. The axis of the horseshoe points towards the midsummer sunrise. The whole area was obviously a centre of great ceremonial activity and there are a number of monuments, massive earthworks, and over 300 burial mounds within a relatively small area. Little is known about the Bronze-Age society that organised such a vast undertaking, but there was no connection with the Druids.

Open all year, daily. Closed Xmas and New Year.

STOURTON HOUSE FLOWER GARDEN
WILTSHIRE. 3 MILES (5KM) NW OF MERE, ON A303
TEL: 01747 840417

Set in the attractive village of Stourton, the house has more than 4 acres (1.5ha) of beautifully maintained flower gardens. Many grass paths lead through varied and colourful shrubs, trees and plants; Stourton House also specialises in unusual plants, many of which are for sale. The garden is also well known for its dried flowers and collection of over 250 different hydrangeas.

Open Apr–Nov, certain days. Also open Dec–Mar for plant/dried flower sales.

SWINDON
WILTSHIRE. TOWN OFF M4, 70 MILES (113KM) W OF LONDON

The largest town in Wiltshire and a thriving business centre, part of 'Silicon Valley', with many recent office blocks. This was a little market town until 1840s, when New Swindon was built down the hill from the Old Town as a locomotive works, making and repairing engines for the new railways. About 300 cottages were built for the workforce, plus a church and pubs. Most of it still survives, with the Great Western Railway Museum and one of the workers' cottages fitted out as it was in the 19th century (see below and page 81).

The old and new towns have expanded and joined, with a big modern shopping centre. There are huge business parks: Windmill Hill with its 18th-century brick windmill, and Greenbridge to the north-east with three statues by Elisabeth Frink. At Shaw Ridge there is a coloured statue of Diana Dors, who was born locally.

The Old Town has its best buildings around the market square, with a Greek-style town hall of 1853 and Georgian houses. Most of the town is Victorian or modern; Swindon has a Museum and Art Gallery and the Swindon and Cricklade Railway.

Great Western Railway Museum
FARINGDON RD
TEL: 01793 466555

The museum is in the Great Western Railway Village in Swindon, once one of the busiest railway towns in Britain, and now has a fascinating collection of locomotives and other exhibits relating to the GWR. Among the locomotives are the historic *Dean Goods* and *King George V* and a replica of the broad-gauge locomotive *North Star*. There is a

*g*azetteer

comprehensive display of nameplates, models, posters and tickets and other railway paraphernalia, and the 'Return to Swindon' exhibition celebrates Swindon's Railway Works and Village, complete with recreated Railway Workshop displays. Plans are underway for a new, enlarged Museum on the Swindon GWR Works Site.

Open all year, daily, certain times. Closed Good Fri, Xmas and New Year.

The museum contains displays of local history, from pre-history through archaeology to the present day. The art gallery has pictures by important British 20th-century artists, including Moore, Sutherland, Wadsworth and Lowry.

Open all year, daily, certain times. Closed Good Fri and Xmas.

Museum & Art Gallery
BATH RD
TEL: 01793 493188

This restored foreman's house is furnished as a typical working-class home at the turn of the century. It was originally part of the model village built in Bath stone by the GWR for its workers.

Open all year, certain times. Closed Saturdays, Good Fri and Xmas.

Railway Village House
34 FARINGDON RD (ADJACENT TO GWR MUSEUM)
TEL: 01793 466553

On Spring Bank Holiday locals celebrate Woolsack Day by racing up Tetbury's steep Gumstool Hill carrying heavy sacks of wool. More leisurely strollers will enjoy delightful streets of mellow buildings, especially in the old Market Place called The Chipping. Additional attractions are the Police Bygones Museum in Long Street, and arguably the most elegant 18th-century church in the Cotswolds.

TETBURY
GLOUCESTERSHIRE. SMALL TOWN ON A433, 10 MILES (16KM) SW OF CIRENCESTER.

Built in 1576, this unspoilt Elizabethan house contains some stained glass from the 16th century and earlier, and some good furniture and tapestries. The owner during the Civil War was a Parliamentarian, and the house also contains Cromwellian relics. In more recent years, the house has been the location for *Grace and Favour* the sequel to the television series *Are You Being Served?*, *Poirot*, *The House of Elliot* and *Noel's House Party*. There is a Shakespeare Week in July. Tours of the house, conducted by the owner or members of his family, are enlivened by many stories of ghosts and the supernatural.

Open May–Sep, certain days and times. Also Etr Sun & Mon. Other days by appointment only.

Chavenage
2 MILES (3KM) NW OF TETBURY SIGNPOSTED OFF A46/B4014
TEL: 01666 502329 & 01453 832700

Situated in the celebrated Wye Valley, Tintern was immortalised by William Wordsworth's poem and is internationally known for its Cistercian abbey founded in 1131. The great abbey church, rebuilt in the 13th century, is one of Britain's most impressive monastic ruins, with

TINTERN PARVA
MONMOUTHSHIRE. VILLAGE ON A466, 4 MILES (6KM) N OF CHEPSTOW

Tintern Abbey, inspiration for Wordsworth's poem on the relationship of man and nature

superb east and west windows. There are exhibitions and rail memorabilia at the former Victorian railway station, which has been imaginatively converted; there is also a crafts complex, and Offa's Dyke and the Wye Valley are popular with walkers.

(See also Picnic site: Tintern Railway Station, pages 83–4.)

picnic site

A short distance from one of the most romantic of monastic ruins, this picnic site is something of a curiosity. Located in a beautiful wooded valley, in what was once the branch line station for Tintern Parva, much remains to remind the visitor of the age of steam.

HOW TO GET THERE

The village of Tintern Parva is on the A466, between Chepstow and Monmouth. From the village proceed north along the A466 for about ½ mile (1km) before following the sign to turn right into the pay-and-display car park at the picnic site.

FACILITIES

There is a footpath adjacent to the car park, with two old railway carriages converted into Tintern Information Centre (subject to seasonal opening).
A signal box has been converted into a craft shop.
The Information Centre houses a small exhibition of railway memorabilia.
There is a buffet restaurant in a converted station building (subject to seasonal opening).
Toilets, picnic tables and drinking water are available at the picnic site. The Wye Valley Walk leads into Tintern village.

Railway enthusiasts are sure to enjoy a picnic at Tintern Station

Tintern Railway Station picnic site, set amid the beautiful scenery of the Wye Valley, is built around the platforms of the old branch line that used to serve the neighbouring village. The remaining buildings have been put to good use, and together with the carriages that still stand in a siding, the site retains something of the atmosphere of the country railway station.

RAILWAY ATTRACTIONS

The buffet and restaurant are decorated with relics from the great days of the railways, while the signal box on the other side of the line is now a craft shop. The two carriages are painted in that distinctively old-fashioned maroon; one houses an exhibition about the station and railways in

general, and the other is the local information centre. The site is also on the Wye Valley Walk, which links Chepstow with Hay, and there is a map explaining the route and its attractions.

HISTORIC BUILDINGS

Tintern village, less than 1 mile (1.5 km) away, is dominated by the remarkable ruin of Tintern Abbey, celebrated in a famous poem by William Wordsworth. Once the wealthiest of the Welsh monasteries, it owes its secluded position on the River Wye to the severe notions of the Cistercian order, and its grandeur to the lords of Chepstow Castle. The Abbey is a fine example of 13th-century Decorated style, and much of the fine nave still stands. (See Tintern Parva, page 81.)

The colourful signals are now fixed but vividly recall the days of steam

CLOSE BY

Almost opposite the entrance to the picnic site is the entrance to Wye Herbs, where home-grown herbs are on sale. About 6 miles (9.5 km) to the south of Tintern is the estuarine town of Chepstow, with its fine castle, and 10 miles (17 km) to the north is the charming market town of Monmouth, with a unique medieval stone gate. To the north-east is the ancient Forest of Dean with its caves and steam railway (see page 35), and along the road to Gloucester on the banks of the Severn are several interesting small towns, including Westbury-on-Severn with its formal Dutch Garden.

TROWBRIDGE–ULEY

The county town of Wiltshire, although not large, has been an important cloth-making town from medieval times and has Victorian mill buildings and many Georgian stone houses, some large and grand. There is a pretty 15th-century church (much restored) and many late 19th-century churches and chapels, as well as local museums.

A wealth of interest in this old weaving village includes a church exemplifying Victorian High Church principles; delightful houses and cottages around the green; and two notable prehistoric sites to the north-west. Hetty Pegler's Tump is a large chambered long barrow (see below) – it is advisable to take a torch. Uley Bury Hill Fort is an Iron-Age camp with splendid views.

This 180-ft (55-m) long barrow is known as Hetty Pegler's Tump. The neolithic burial mound is about 85 feet (26m) wide and is surrounded by a dry-built wall. It contains a central passage, built of stone, and three burial chambers.
Open at any reasonable time.

TROWBRIDGE
WILTSHIRE. TOWN OFF A363, 8 MILES (13KM) SE OF BATH

ULEY
GLOUCESTERSHIRE. VILLAGE ON B4066, 2 MILES (3KM) E OF DURSLEY.

Uley Tumulus
3½ MILES (5.5KM) NE OF DURSLEY ON B4066

Uley from across the valley

St Andrew's Well, in the grounds of the Bishop's Palace, is one of the wells which gave the city its name

WARMINSTER
WILTSHIRE. TOWN OFF A36, 6 MILES (10KM) SE OF FROME

▶ Warminster consists of one main street, with a mixture of brick, stone and timber-framed buildings, ranging from the 16th to 19th centuries. The imitation Jacobean town hall dates from 1832, and there is a pretty 15th-century church and a grammar school of 1707: the downs are close by. The town has a local museum.

WELLS
SOMERSET. CITY ON A39, 17 MILES (24KM) S OF BRISTOL

▶ England's smallest city, with one of the finest cathedrals and bishop's palaces. The perfect market square seems to have every type and date of building, with two medieval gatehouses, one leading to the cathedral, the other to the bishop's palace. The palace has the most picturesque setting: walled, moated and with old trees. It includes a 13th-century chapel, ruins of the huge hall, and the Henderson Rooms. The wells or springs which gave the town its name are in the garden.

The most memorable parts of the cathedral are the 13th-century west front, and, inside, the huge 1330s scissor-braces inserted to stop the tower falling down. There are quantities of fine fittings and monuments,

and a famous view up the stone steps to the chapter house.

Vicar's Close is the most complete medieval street in Europe, built in the mid-14th century. The rest of the town is pretty, with a fine 15th-century church dedicated to St Cuthbert.

Close to the cathedral is the moated bishop's palace. The early part of the palace, the bishop's chapel and the ruins of the banqueting hall date from the 13th century; the undercroft remains virtually unchanged from this time. There are several state rooms and a long gallery which houses portraits of former Bishops. The palace is ringed with fortifications as well as the moat, and access can only be gained through the 14th-century gatehouse. The name of the city is taken from the wells in the palace grounds. Events include Sealed Knot battle re-enactments and Classics West open air concerts. Please telephone for details.

Open Etr Sat–Oct, certain days.

The Bishop's Palace
HENDERSON ROOMS, NEXT TO
CATHEDRAL OFF THE MARKET
SQUARE
TEL: 01749 678691

WESTBURY

WILTSHIRE. TOWN ON A350, 4 MILES (6KM) S OF TROWBRIDGE

A woollen cloth town from medieval times, with a large market place and pleasant Georgian houses, everything small-scale. The town hall was built in 1815, and the indoor swimming pool of 1887 is supposedly the oldest still in use in Britain. A museum is housed in a restored woollen cloth mill; a 400-ft (122-m) chimney to the north was built for a large cement factory. The Woodland Park is to the west, and the Westbury White Horse (see Bratton, page 15) is near by.

Woodland Heritage Museum & Woodland Park

BROKERSWOOD. TURN OFF A36 AT BELL INN, STANDERWICK. FOLLOW BROWN TOURIST INFORMATION SIGNS TEL: 01373 822238 & 823880

Nature walks lead through 80 acres (32ha) of woodlands, with a lake and wildfowl. Facilities include a woodland visitor centre (covering wildlife and forestry), two children's adventure playgrounds, indoor soft play area and guided walks and the Smokey Oak Railway. Barbecue sites and fishing permits are available.

Park open all year, daily. Museum open all year, certain days and times.

WESTON-SUPER-MARE

TOWN ON A370, 18 MILES (28KM) SW OF BRISTOL.

This large seaside resort is situated on the northern approaches to Bridgwater Bay, on the Bristol Channel. Famous for its miles of dark golden sand (the tide here goes out an exceptionally long way) and donkey rides, its development as a resort began with the building of the Royal Hotel in 1811. The railway arrived in 1841 and the Royal Potteries were founded six years later; the English end of the transatlantic cable came ashore here in 1885. Many Victorian buildings remain today.

Weston Woods lie on a ridge to the north, with a toll road running through them. To the north is Worlebury Camp, an Iron Age hill-fort situated on a headland. The town's Woodspring Museum has local displays, and there is also an International Helicopter Museum (see below). Recently opened is the popular Sea Life Centre, featuring a display of British marine creatures.

International Helicopter Museum

WESTON AIRPORT, LOCKING MOOR ROAD (ON THE A371, ON THE OUTSKIRTS OF TOWN) TEL: 01934 635227

This unique collection includes more than 50 helicopters and autogyros, as well as exhibits of models, photographs and components illustrating how the aircraft work. There is a ride simulator, and on some Sundays between March and October 'Open Cockpit' days are held when visitors can try out the pilot's seat of a real helicopter, and receive instruction from museum guides.

Helicopters from this display also feature in the 'Weston Super Holidays' which take place on the seafront and feature flying and static displays of up to 50 helicopters. Recent additions include G-Lynx, the world's fastest helicopter, and a Russian 'Hind' attack helicopter.

Open all year, certain days. Closed Xmas and New Year.

Opposite: Donkeys on the beach at Weston-Super-Mare

This large arboretum was started in 1820 and contains one of the finest and most important collection of trees and shrubs in the world. There are 18,000 of them, planted from 1829 to the present day, covering 600 acres (243ha) of landscaped Cotswold countryside. The visitor can follow 17 miles (27km) of waymarked trails or simply sit in a leafy glade and admire some of the great varieties of trees and shrubs which provide interest and colour throughout the year, even in winter, when the distinctive barks of the birches and maple are visible. Magnificent displays of rhododendrons, azaleas, magnolias and the wild flowers of silkwood can be seen in spring. There is a Visitor Centre with an exhibition, shop, and interesting video programme. The arboretum is managed by the Forestry Commission.

Open all year, daily.

A handsome stone village with a fine medieval church. Westwood Manor (see page 92) is a perfect stone manor house, late medieval and early 18th century, with a topiary garden. Iford Manor (see page 92) is an attractive Georgian stone mansion, with fascinating gardens ornamented with old Italian sculpture.

WESTONBIRT ARBORETUM
*GLOUCESTERSHIRE. 3 MILES
(5KM) S OF TETBURY ON A433
TEL: 01666 880220*

WESTWOOD
*WILTSHIRE. VILLAGE OFF A363,
1 MILE (2KM) SW OF
BRADFORD-ON-AVON.*

Walk

Grid ref: SU98719

INFORMATION

The walk is about 3 miles (5km) long.
Level ground with one gentle hill.
Several stiles.
No road walking.
New Inn in Winterbourne Monkton has a garden with play equipment; also pub, restaurant and café in Avebury.
Windmill Hill suitable for picnics.

START

Winterbourne Monkton is 1 mile (1.5km) north of Avebury. On entering the village look for a turning to the left marked Manor Farm and Church. Follow the road through the farm, past the church. Immediately on the left next to the church is a concrete yard where you can park.

The steep climb up Windmill Hill can be very bracing on a windy day, but combined with a visit to Avebury, this walk will provide an interesting and rewarding day out.

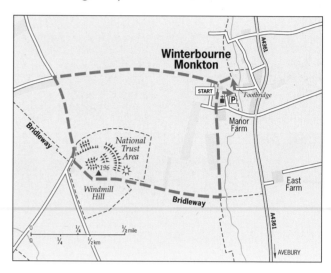

DIRECTIONS

Turn left out of the yard and on the corner turn right down a footpath which reaches a footbridge. (To visit the village of Winterbourne Monkton cross the bridge.)

Avebury stone circle

Continue straight on to the left of the footbridge over rough ground to reach a stile. Follow the direction of the arrow across the field to another stile. Do not cross this stile, but turn to the left and head for a stile with a signpost on

the opposite side of the field. Cross this and drop down the bank on to a farm track and turn right. Continue along the track for about ¾ mile (1km), passing a barn on the right, to a junction of several paths, then turn left. Reach a stile leading on to Windmill Hill. Head straight up to the top where there are fenced-off mounds (good views). Proceed in the same general direction, past the mounds, to leave the area over a stile behind the last mound. Continue until the path becomes a tarmac track at the bottom of the hill. Go through the gate and almost immediately turn

left into a field. Cross the field and continue to follow the footpath signs, crossing over a further four stiles and muddy farm tracks. Pass the farm on your right and continue ahead to the road. Turn right to reach the car park.

Windmill Hill

About 5,000 years ago Windmill Hill was occupied by a large neolithic settlement and excavations of the site by Alexander Keiller in the 1920s yielded rich pickings. The vast amount of bones (human and animal), beads, pots, flint implements etc that were found in the ditches gave a clear picture of the community's way of life, and this is well documented in the

Alexander Keiller Museum in Avebury. The 20 or so acres (8ha) enclosed by three circles of ditches and banks are now in the care of the National Trust or English Heritage.

Avebury

A mile (1.5km) from the start of the walk lies the fascinating village of Avebury and a visit here before or after the walk provides enough of interest to fill the rest of the day easily. As well

Part of the route follows a broad track through farmland

as the famous stones, there is Avebury Manor (National Trust) and the thatched Great Barn, housing a shop and the Museum of Wiltshire Folk Life. There are displays on dairying and the work of the thatcher, saddler, shepherd and wheelwright. The Alexander Keiller Museum has displays of archaeological finds. (See also pages 5–6).

WHAT TO LOOK OUT FOR

On a clear day the stone circles of Avebury can be seen from the top of Windmill Hill. Listen for skylarks and watch for kestrels on your route.

Westwood Manor
1½ MILES (2.5KM) SW OF
BRADFORD-ON-AVON, OFF
B3109
TEL: 01225 863374

The property of the National Trust, this late 15th-century stone manor house has some particularly fine Jacobean plasterwork. The house, which is situated by the parish church, was altered in 1610 but still retains its late Gothic and Jacobean windows. Outside there is a superb modern topiary garden.

Open Apr–Oct, certain days and times.

Iford Manor Gardens
2½ MILES (4KM) SW OF
BRADFORD-ON-AVON

Occupying a steep hillside above the languorous River Frome, the fascinating gardens of Iford Manor are a subtle blend of Italianate layout and English planting. This was the garden created by the distinguished architect and landscape designer, Harold Peto – a partner of the turn-of-the-century country house architect, Ernest George, and a great influence on his young assistant, Edwin Lutyens. The topography of Iford lent itself to the strong architectural framework of terraces, and the predominant theme of the design is Italian, with plantings of cypress, juniper, box and yew interspersed with stone sarcophagi, urns, marble seats and statues, columns and loggias. The whole is presented with stunning light and shade effects that are almost theatrical.

The garden is entered by a loggia at the south-east corner of the Tudor house. Across the paved courtyard is a semi-circular pond, and Peto set an Italian Renaissance window (with its original glass) into the loggia, while the balconies above are wrought iron, dating from 1450. Worn steps lead up to the second terrace and the conservatory where two ancient fluted columns stand. Below the flight of steps that takes you up to the lawn are a pair of Italian marble lions dating from 1200. Here the planting complements the grey stone, with wisteria and other climbing plants and purple sage predominating. Brighter colours are also in evidence, with the pink of escallonias, red roses, gladioli and cotinus catching the eye, and with the Chilean glory flower growing on the steps. Peto created a small pool at this level, planted with potentillas, while shallow steps lead to a paved area overflowing with ladies' mantle and punctuated by day lilies, shaded by a weeping birch. The Blue Pool has a Romanesque bas-relief depicting a woman riding a lion set into the wall, and the pool itself is surrounded by honeysuckle and pink roses.

The Great Terrace runs from a curved seat at its western end to a small 18th-century tea-house at the other, with senecio rambling over the paving and rosemary growing in the middle of a millstone. The Casita has pink marble columns, a dancing nymph in the inside niche, and a 14th- century Venetian Gothic wheel window, while its courtyards is planted with lavender, artemisias and rosemary. On the south side of the terrace a bronze wolf suckles Romulus and Remus,

and the bed below the statue contains irises, berberis and meadow rue. In the woodland to the north, the owners, Mr and Mrs Cartwright-Hignett, are constructing a Japanese water garden begun by Harold Peto, and beyond the Roman sarcophagus is an 18th-century tea-house. Through a charming arbour of berberis, beeches and laburnum are the cloisters, built by Peto in the Italian Romanesque style to house antique fragments.

Open Apr–Oct, on selected days.

A neolithic ceremonial monument of c2300 BC, consisting of six concentric rings of timber posts, now marked by concrete piles. The long axis of the rings, which are oval, points to the rising sun on Midsummer Day.

Open all reasonable times. (See also Amesbury, page 5.)

WOODHENGE
Wiltshire. 1½ miles (2.5km) N of Amesbury, off A345 just S of Durrington

This Mendip village is famous for the limestone caves from which the River Axe appears. The large caves are accessible (see below), and have a famous echo. A fairground museum is located in the old papermill; paper has been produced here since the 17th century.

WOOKEY HOLE
Somerset. Village off A371, 2 miles (3km) NW of Wells

The caves are the main feature of Wookey Hole. Visitors enjoy a ½-mile (1-km) tour through the Chambers, accompanied by a knowledgeable guide who points out the amazing stalagmites and stalactites, including the famous Witch of Wookey. The guides use remote-controlled lighting to highlight geological features and illustrate the history and myths associated with the caves. Visitors also take in the Victorian Papermill, at one time amongst the largest handmade papermills in Europe, which sold exquisite paper all over the world. Also in the mill are the Fairground Memories, historically important late 19th-century and early 20th-century fairground rides, and the Magical Mirror Maze, which is an enclosed passage of multiple-image mirrors creating an illusion of endless reflections. After the fun of the maze, visitors move on to a typical Old Penny Arcade where they can purchase old pennies to operate the original machines.

Open all year, daily. Closed Xmas week.

Wookey Hole Caves & Papermill
Tel: 01749 672243

On the edge of the Somerset Levels, the main street of Yatton is lined with stone houses and cottages. The handsome church has a fine 14th-century tower (the spire was added in the 15th century) and a magnificent late 15th-century elaborate porch. The Newton Chapel has effigies of Sir John and Lady Newton, who paid for the late 15th-century rebuilding of the church.

YATTON
Somerset. Village on B3133, 4miles (6km) S of Clevedon

LISTINGS

CONTACTS AND ADDRESSES

TOURIST INFORMATION CENTRES

Amesbury, Redworth House, Flower Lane
Tel: 01980 622833

Bath, Abbey Chambers, Abbey Church Yard
Tel: 01225 477101

Bradford-on-Avon, 34 Silver Street
Tel: 01225 865797

Bristol, St Nicholas Church, St Nicholas
Street. Tel: 0117 926 0767

Cheddar, The Gorge
Tel: 01934 744071

Chippenham, The Citadel, Bath Road
Tel: 01249 706333

Cirencester, Corn Hall, Market Place
Tel: 01285 654180

Glastonbury, The Tribunal, 9 High Street
Tel: 01458 832954

Malmesbury, Town Hall, Market Lane
Tel: 01666 823748

Marlborough, George Lane Car Park
Tel: 01672 513989

Melksham, Church Street
Tel: 01225 707424

Mere, The Square
Tel: 01747 861211

Somerset Visitor Centre, M5 South
nr Axbridge
Tel: 01934 750833

Swindon, 37 Regent Street
Tel: 01793 530328

Tetbury, 33 Church Street
Tel: 01666 503552

Trowbridge, St Stephen's Place
Tel: 01225 777054

Warminster, Central Car Park
Tel: 01985 218548

Wells, Town Hall, Market Place
Tel: 01749 672552

Westbury, The Library, Edward Street
Tel: 01373 827158

Weston-Super-Mare, Beach Lawns
Tel: 01934 626838

Some Tourist Information Centres have
seasonal opening times. Please telephone
to check.

The AA Hotel Booking Service

This new service provided exclusively for AA
personal members is a FREE, fast and easy
way to find a place to stay for your short
break, business trip or holiday. With your
membership number to hand, call the AA
Hotel Booking Service on 0990 050505.

INDEX

ACKNOWLEDGEMENTS

The Automobile Association wishes to thank the following photographers and libraries for their assistance in the preparation of this book.

NATURE PHOTOGRAPHERS LTD 64/5 (R BUSH)
TONY STONE IMAGES front cover picture

The remaining photographs are held in the Association's own library (AA PHOTO LIBRARY) with contributions from:

A BAKER 52, 67, 71, 77; M BIRKITT 14, 79; HILARY BURN 73; S DAY back cover (b); 9, 12, 22, 23, 24, 34, 36/7, 44, 48, 55, 56, 61, 62, 76, 85, 86/7; D FORSS 49; A LAWSON 70, 78; S & O MATTHEWS 5, 8, 60; E MEACHER back cover (a) 11, 18, 28, 68/9, 75, 89; R NEWTON back cover (c); NEIL RAY 7, 15, 16, 17, 27; M SHORT 32, 47, 58/9, 72, 74, 90, 91; T SOUTER 20/1, R SURMAN 51; J A TIMS front cover inset; W VOYSEY 19, 39, 42; H WILLIAMS 26, 41, 84.